1907
THE · NEW · HARTFORD
FREE · PUBLIC · LIBRARY

TOWN OF
· 1738 ·
NEW HARTFORD

NEW HARTFORD, CONN.

Added _____

Class _____ No. _____

Gift of
_____ William Franklin _____

The Painter's Composition Handbook

The
Painter's Composition
Handbook

Jan Herring

Book Designed by
Mandeville Hutton Zabriskie, Jr.

Acknowledgements to
Mary Nell Gentry
Charlotte Hays

Second Edition

Published by
Poor-Henry Publishing Company
P. O. BOX 156, CLINT, TEXAS 79836

Printed by
Guynes Printing Company
EL PASO, TEXAS

In Appreciation

For almost twenty years I have had the opportunity to observe
Jan Herring's devotion to art and her development
to an accomplished artist. With undiminished singleness of purpose she
has continued probing into things visually apprehended and
conceived in terms of the esthetics we inherited from the great
masters of the past. The results of her labors are now
gathered in their theoretic framework on the pages of this book.
It would seem to me that in the technology of picture
construction her disquisitions are presented with greater acuity and
clarity than can be found in most of the writings on the subject.
The treatise on materials and color has all the virtues inherent in a
profound knowledge of the subject. It is my opinion that
the serious student will find in this manual a valuable source
of information and inspiration.

FREDERIC TAUBES
HAVERSTRAW, NEW YORK

Contents

Contents

Dedicated to
FREDERIC TAUBES

1

Introduction

PURPOSE OF THE HANDBOOK

M ANY THOUSANDS OF WORDS have been written on the subject of composition. The works of the masters and contemporaries have been scrutinized, analyzed and categorized in an attempt to establish an identification of the principles of structuring a painting. Some basic, indisputable facts run through these various manuscripts, yet the student is bewildered over the apparent ambiguities and vagaries that dominate these treatises. Many critics and authors keep the reader in a quandary as to their meaning of words and phrases. Confusion prevails. The student in need of answers finds himself frustrated and disillusioned. How can the serious student or teacher, for that matter, sift the facts from the fiction? How is he to identify the fallacy of the well-turned phrase? Where can he find a reasonable instrument that can be applied logically to further his understanding of composition?

It seems appropriate to present the student with a foundation based on constant, recurring principles rather than fill him with useless theory and meaningless phrases. I am aware that the modern concept of composition makes no allowance for "constants", yet my experiences as a painter and teacher contradict this theory. Despite the continuous fluctuation of ever changing standards of art, there are recurring recognizable principles in the work of the ancients to the moderns.

The aim of this book is to establish these general principles in simple terms that are applicable to all forms of expression without delving specifically into the philosophy of art forms. It is not my intention to condemn or refute other approaches to art. I am addressing the student who is seeking a workable procedure for structuring a sound composition.

It does not seem plausible to discuss intuitive knowledge or creative urges on these pages. Being primarily a creative painter myself, I know from experience the inestimable value of the elusive quality of the creative process, but my experience as a teacher demands that I present the student with some concrete tools of application that can direct him into a sound working procedure. His talent and creative processes will work for him once he has been disciplined into a logical and reasonable path of development.

A painter must be programmed to a discipline of organized thought if his creativity is to be effectively expressed. Discipline is primary in all areas of the creative arts and does not exclude the painter from the group as an exception to the rule. A painting is not a painting simply because a person has felt a creative urge stirring within him and proceeds to do "his thing". A good painting is the result of clear, concise thinking with the skillfull application of the craft.

The poet must first learn the metrical form, the rules and structure of his craft before he can expect to create a poem. The metrical rhythm ties the words together and makes them function, just as the composition binds the pictorial idea into a solid visual experience. The astute professional painter realizes that his creative energies respond to discipline. This is not to say that the creativity must be suppressed by rigid rules. On the contrary, the painter has always been granted poetic license. The error is in the student's assuming an undisciplined approach before he has learned compositional craftsmanship. Once good habit patterns have been established, conscious thought to structure and technique can be disregarded and the painter can proceed uninhibited by rules.

The student who seems to possess an innate understanding of composition is the rare student indeed. The progress of this student is rapid because of his natural sense of balance, color and form. The technique of painting is soon learned with the practical application of paint. The majority of art students lack this great gift and the road to success is not smooth. It is generally assumed that if a would-be-painter lacks this compositional knowledge, he cannot be taught. Personally, I do not agree with this deduction. Composition can be taught in the sense that the student can be given an instrument to guide him in developing his skill and sensitivity to balance, line, color, form, light and shade.

The position of a teacher is to lead the student into experiences that will enable him to teach himself how to draw, to paint, to construct a painting. One approach to this is to make guide lines and establish rules. These rules are made from a gathering of experiences. This is not to say that a rule is absolute. On the contrary, a rule is useful only in a learning process. There are no absolutes. The procedures presented in this handbook are intended to guide the student into a disciplined thought process developed from a study of the craft of structuring a painting. *Freedom of artistic expression can only be gained through such discipline of thought and through the application of sound craftsmanship.*

HOW TO USE THE HANDBOOK

For the last several years, I have had a compositional experiment in the field, working with hundreds of students in all phases of development. I have given them a simple tool — the alphabet — as the structural foundation for their paintings and controlled their learning process by strict attention to the rules. The result has been most gratifying to me as a teacher, as well as for the students.

Many of the students, some teachers themselves, have asked me to put this theory into book form for use as a reference guide that would be available to a more extensive audience. For this reason, I have organized the material into a handbook. The manuscript naturally has limitations for I have no intention of teaching the student how to draw or paint. It is intended to establish a foundation of constant compositional principles. Once learned, these principles will enable the student to proceed with confidence and develop his intuitive creative instincts in a natural progression.

The book has been designed in a schematic arrangement of practical exercises. The innovations are intended to be employed as a workbook and the suggested exercises followed and conscientiously practiced. Each phase of composition is explored individually. The student may spend as much time on each phase as he deems necessary, proceeding to the following section when he completely understands the presented problems.

The last section is devoted to the actual painting of pictures. A brief discussion of color and technique of painting has been included to facilitate the painting exercises. All of the knowledge gained from the preceding sections is gathered together in a composite idea, allowing the student to apply, with organized thought, the principles of composition.

The student will find his comprehension growing with each procedure if this book is used according to its intentional design. The teacher will discover an organized step-by-step teaching plan that can be applied to any age group or any level of development. The experienced painter can improve his analytical insight to his own work and the knowledge gained will enable him to correct his structural errors.

2

Clarification of the Principles of Composition

IDENTIFICATION OF COMPOSITION

COMPOSITION IS LINE, form, balance, color, rhythm and space. A composition is all of these factors and more. It is a theme, an idea housed in an abstract structure.

Line is an element of design, a tool of decoration, an instrument to build form. Form is an enclosed shape developed by line and color. Color is the visual impact of the reflection of pigment on the retina of the eye; a tool of the painter to control emotion and rhythm. Balance is the result of the composing of line, form and color around a central axis point. *Controlled space is the structural force that binds all of the components into a solid, unified whole.*

Now, what is to be done with these bits and pieces of information? It seems reasonable to delve into each part individually and discover its usefulness and methods of application.

You, the student, must be cognizant of the fact that the theme, the subject idea, has nothing whatsoever to do with the structure of a painting. Structure is identified by the dispersion of light and shade on a surface, forming a pattern that is stretched to the outer limits of the painting surface. This structural principle of chiaroscuro is a dominant, continuously recurring principle through all phases of art, past and present. We must assume it is a "constant" principle. We must also recognize that this abstract structure, this pattern of light and shade, supersedes all other principles of composition.

Before the student can comprehend the total scope of structure, he must first be made aware of symbolism (line), form (positive and negative shape) and the central axis (focal point) as components of composition.

This section is devoted to a discussion of these factors. It is intended to give the student the practical side of compositional theory and point the way for developing his skill in the application of those basic principles. It enables the student to know himself; that is, to discover what he understands innately and what must be learned through applied study. Once this is known, the student can extend his thinking into a personalized process suited to his creative spirit.

LINE

Line is an impression on a surface. Line is straight, curved, static or dynamic but it makes no sense at all until it is placed within the borders of our sense of recognizable form. Once this relationship is established, line assumes an emotional force that can be directed and controlled by the painter.

Each time we look at nature with the intention of conveying its illusions into paint, we are confronted with the selection of line that will best convey our meaning. The essence of line can best be understood when it is divided into three general categories—curved line, dot or static line and straight line.

LINE AND THE PICTURE PLANE

The size and shape of the picture plane is often neglected as a contributing factor to composition. The four periphery lines of the surface must necessarily be given the utmost consideration. The student must consciously select the shape and size to coincide with the emotional intent of the composition.

Shape has an emotion, an attitude depending upon its placement in space. Understand that the closer the four periphery lines of a canvas come to equalization, the more static is the framed shape. The farther these lines are extended from each other, the more dynamic is the created form. A 16″ x 20″ standard size canvas, the outside measurements being almost equal in length, will house a composition designed to conform to its squarish shape. The emotional response to such a shape will be that of boredom. It imparts a static situation unless the composition is constructed with awareness of its innate emotional form. In other words, a 16″ x 20″ is a dull canvas compared to the dramatic attitude presented by that of a 15″ x 30″.

A long narrow canvas will allow for extensive exploration of the dynamic forces because its dimensions are already dramatic. If this shape is placed in a horizontal position, the emotional attitude is one of repose and lends a static feeling to the form. Place the narrow shape in an upright position and it immediately assumes a surging power.

It should be noted that the vertical composition is the least difficult to organize into a composition. Perhaps this is because we are upright creatures and our eye is naturally disposed to this position. It seems difficult for the human eye to move from side to side. The eye must be encouraged to do so by deliberate means.

Consider the size itself. A miniature painting may possess greatness of quality but its mere size seems to hold it into a lesser artistic effort. True or not, the impact of the size is limited. Enlarge the size and you increase the visual impact. However, beware of overemphasis on this point. Once a painting exceeds the normal bounds of easel painting, you are in the field of mural painting and can no longer identify with your profession.

It is imperative that the student be aware that the four periphery lines of the canvas surface form the beginning of his structure. All innovations imprinted on the interior surface must actively relate to these four lines. The space held by the picture plane must be totally consumed and stretched to the limit of the outer boundary lines. You must tie up the shape as if you were binding it with string so that it is a tight, solid, compact whole.

ART OF DRAWING

A few words should be devoted to the novice in the art of drawing. The art student is too often told that he does not need to know how to draw in order to learn to paint. Such a theory is dangerous when it is adopted by the gullible, eager novice. The ability to draw well is a major necessity for the painter, even if a line, as such, never appears on the surface of his painting. A painter must know his subject before he can effectively convey the illusion in paint. Such knowledge can be gained only through training the eye to see and the hand to record. Expressive, sensitive drawing can only result from years of sincere and continuous effort. The clean, deft skill with the pencil and brush will always be felt over the hesitant and weak delineation.

Convincing distortion of an object or figure has always been an accepted device of the painter. The contemporary thought does not demand an absoluteness of rendering but allows the painter complete freedom of expression. In this post-Cezanne period, the painter is not bound to stylization of his time. Scientific perspective can be forgotten or at least set aside. The contemporary painter seeks out the essence, the expression of his subject, with complete freedom of choice. A drawing that captures the attitude of the object or figure is much more expressive than the drawing that employs absolute mechanical representation. Some painters suffer from a compulsive desire to depict every detail of an object and find it difficult to separate themselves from the tyranny of exactitude.

There are many fine books available to the curious student. One of the best is *The Natural Way to Draw* by Kimon Nicolaides, which presents a rather unique system of study aimed at the development of the essential qualities inherent to fine draftsmanship. Seldom have I found a student who has not been able, with serious application of this book, to master the elementary mechanics of drawing within a few months. He then has the means of putting down with some degree of accuracy, relative proportions, outlines and masses of shape; he understands how to place an object firmly on a table and to make it turn and stand in space. Such drawing is not the expressive, fluid line of the professional hand, but it is a beginning. Continuous adaptation of the principles of the book will bring him to eventual mastery of his craft.

POSITIVE AND NEGATIVE SHAPE

Positive shape versus negative shape: what does this comparatively simple-sounding phrase mean? *Postive shape refers to a space completely enclosed by a contour.* Therefore, the opposite or negative shape refers to unenclosed space. Often one reads that positive shape is the object or subject matter and negative shape is background. Both definitions are correct. The problem is not so much defining the terms, but how to recognize negative areas and transform them into positive shapes because a painting must be a completeness, a whole expression. *All space on the painting surface must be positive.* This fact is often misunderstood. No matter in what style the painter has chosen to work, the challenge is to encompass all of the allotted space with some form of contour and hold that space within the boundary lines of the painting.

A well-knit composition holds the eye within the surface of the picture plane. The eye enters the painting at the focal point, travels over the surface and back again to the focal point, where the eye leaves the painting. The eye must never be forced out of the picture by negative areas, but rather controlled by positive space.

How do you create positive space? With enclosed line, texture or color. Simple? Relatively, yes. Once space itself is understood, the converting of the negative areas into positive shapes is relatively simple.

IDENTIFYING NEGATIVE SHAPE

The unperceptive student invariably will fill the periphery areas of the canvas with paraphernalia, such as a rock in one corner, a bush in another, a piece of a tree drooping into the picture from some place in outer space. All of these misplaced subjects seem to surround a painted area of nothingness. A road or river, funneling its path out of the picture at the center front periphery, or worse, from the corner, originates from the theory of focal point or entrance into the picture. Rather than draw the eye into the picture, it pulls it out. The river invariably widens at the periphery line, forming a negative shape which causes the eye to leave the painting and the water to end up on the living room floor.

The motif should be concentrated in the middle of the canvas shape, not in the periphery area. The strongest color in your painting must be in the middle ground area. The background and foreground in your painting and all four corners, are held in an understatement to prevent overemphasis of unimportant areas.

The position of negative space can best be understood through visual aids. The illustrations that follow denote the negative areas and explain how to rehabilitate them as positive shape. Keep in mind that before negative space can be rehabilitated into positive space, you must school yourself to recognize the negative areas that are formed by the selection and placement of objects onto a canvas surface.

TYPES OF SHAPE

Designing a painting on a pyramid has long been accepted as a legitimate composition idea. Such a concept is faulty. A pyramid is a symmetrical shape. Its perfect balance brings about inertia, which is crippling to any painting design. The triangular shapes are completely enclosed, forming positive shapes, but they are monotonous and dull. The eye cannot refrain from following each directional line to the points of the triangle, there to be lost in nothingness. If a triangle is built on a periphery line, the eye is projected out of the painting into space.

The perfect circle is another pitfall of the inexperienced painter. Again, it brings on inertia because of its continuous monotony and perfection. If the circle is of any size at all, it seems to be at odds with the rectangle which houses it. The circle can only be effective when it is broken and distorted. Then it becomes an active, useful symbol.

So far, we have considered only the bad shapes. Let's look at the square and the rectangle. Both are excellent in composition. The natural formation of the right angles allows the eye to move freely within the shape. They can actually be so effective as to allow the painter to build his entire composition with these various sizes and shapes. Some contemporary painters have become so entranced with the square that they have devoted a large bulk of their work with respect to the square and rectangle. A few examples: Josef Alber's "Homage to the Square", Abraham Rattner's "Composition with Three Figures" and Mark Rathko's "Orange Over Yellow".

Now consider Edward Hopper, who does not stand in awe of the square and rectangle but a great many of his works are founded upon them with the forms standing parallel to the periphery edge of the canvas. His "Early Morning" and "Rooms by the Sea" are good examples.

Andrew Wyeth is another painter who puts the square and rectangle to good use. His emphasis is always on motif rather than structure but the structure can always be identified by the light and dark pattern. His best work is built with parallel structure blocks. "Chambered Nautilus" is an example. In contrast, study Wyeth's landscapes that are built on triangular structure forms. The resulting funnels carry the eye out of the painting in all directions. Wyeth makes no adjustments to hold these forms into the surface; consequently, he has a very poor percentage of success in this type of compositional structure.

FOCAL POINT

There seems to be a great deal of confusion surrounding the term focal point. The confusion arises from the mistaken idea that focal point and point of interest are the same thing and that if a painting has an entrance for the eye, it must have an exit at a separate point.

A painting certainly must present an entrance point for the eye. The eye must focus on this point, enter the painting and travel about the surface by relying on existing rhythm. The eye is returned to its starting point and leaves the painting by its own volition. This entrance point is also the axis which controls the balance of the composition. This dual point is almost always located slightly below center, right or left.

PERSPECTIVE IN COMPOSITION

The employment of perspective in the pictorial rendering of a painting has many variations of concept as history proves. The Early Christian and Byzantine schools employed a two dimensional arrangement of space by placing objects side by side and on top of each other without showing depth. Such arrangement has a great attraction in our day because it appears to be almost unplanned and innocent. The principle of scientific perspective had its heyday in the Renaissance period where it was fully exploited. Employment of such perspective, utilizing the vanishing point, seemed to be the guiding principle of Renaissance painting structure.

With the entrance of Paul Cezanne, composition innovations became prominent. Cezanne has often been called the "Father of Modern Art" because of his original concept of perspective. Cezanne presented many points of view and eye levels of objects simultaneously. He opened up a new idea in space arrangement by eliminating scientific perspective as a standard form of structure.

As a result, the characteristic features of contemporary paintings seem to emphasize structure over motif. The student today has a free choice of adopting a flat two dimensional space or painting in depth and employing three dimensional principles. He need not consider scientific perspective unless he chooses to do so.

Erle Loran's book, *Cezanne's Compositions*, presents an excellent analysis of the painter's work. It is clear and factual and so well-presented that there is no reason to elaborate upon it here. Let it suffice to say that *Cezanne's Compositions* is on the required reading list.

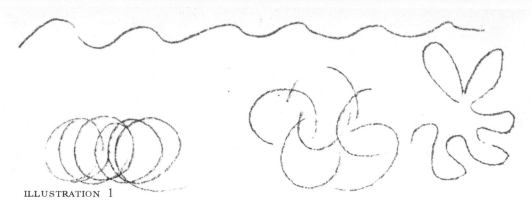

ILLUSTRATION 1

CURVED LINE

The continuous circular line denotes a feeling
of completeness, continuity, and lends
a sense of the serene. Break the circle and
distort it; interlace it with similar movements and
the emotional attitude changes. The
line assumes exuberance, movement and
excitement.

THE DOT OR STATIC LINE

The dot or dash line is inert. It only
begins to function in conjunction with like
symbols. When many such staccato
marks are drawn, the emotional response is one
of agitation or confusion because of its
congested appearance.

STRAIGHT LINE

The straight line, when placed horizontally on a
surface, is static and inert and tends to
recall attributes of peace, quiet and serenity.
When the direction of the line is changed,
it takes on a new personality. Its power magnifies
directly to the degree it is raised on the
surface. Converging line increases the
dramatic response, introduces excitement and
becomes more interesting for the eye to observe.

ILLUSTRATION 2

This drawing illustrates line
in recognizable flower shapes.
The flowers are drawn
with both curved and straight
line with the dot and static
line forming the stamen
of the blooms. The leaves and
stems are expressed by
combining straight and curved
lines but the emotional
impact is more dynamic than in
the flower shapes themselves.

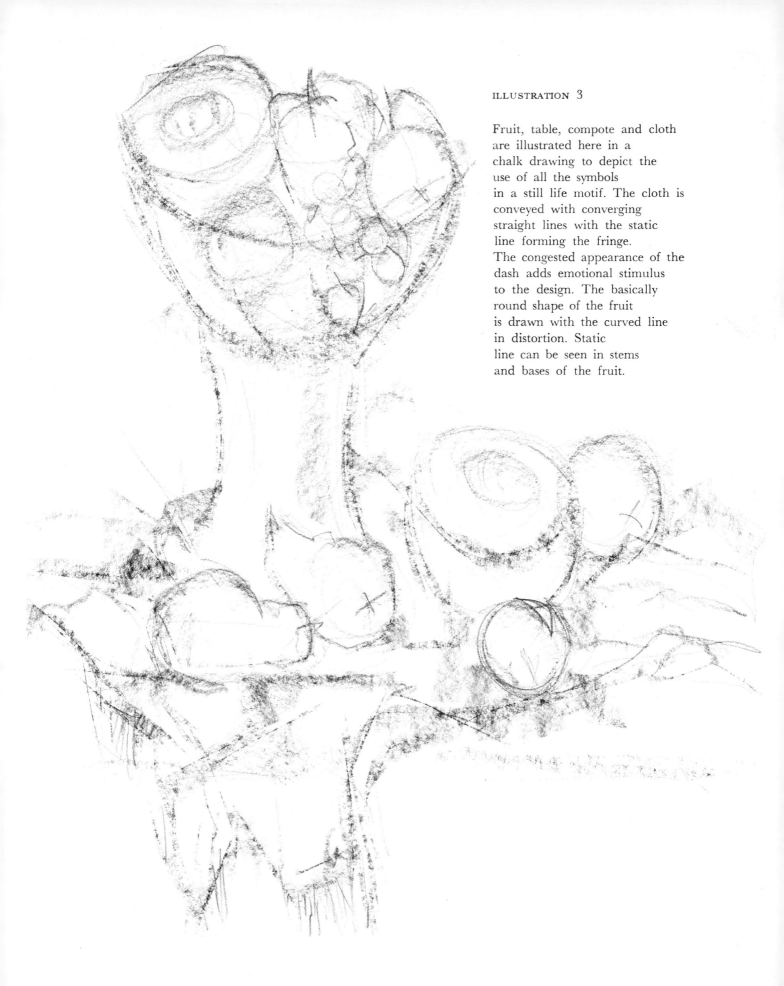

ILLUSTRATION 3

Fruit, table, compote and cloth
are illustrated here in a
chalk drawing to depict the
use of all the symbols
in a still life motif. The cloth is
conveyed with converging
straight lines with the static
line forming the fringe.
The congested appearance of the
dash adds emotional stimulus
to the design. The basically
round shape of the fruit
is drawn with the curved line
in distortion. Static
line can be seen in stems
and bases of the fruit.

ILLUSTRATION 4

A landscape theme has been
drawn utilizing only the
straight line to gain the illusion
of trees and rocks. The
upward thrust of the dramatic
straight line is countered
by the straight line in
horizontal positions. The total
use of straight line symbols
lends an abstract quality
to the drawing.

ILLUSTRATION 5

A head study of a mother with her child
illustrates the predominant use of the
curved symbols to form the main concept of the
drawing. The emotional effect of
peace and serenity is controlled to a great
extent by the abundance of the curved
line symbols. Straight line can be seen as contrast
in the hair, hands, and arms of the
child. The costume of the mother is suggested
by the converging of straight lines over
the curved line of the shoulder. Dots and dashes
are used to portray the eyes and
lashes of both figures. You can also see
the static line in the mouth, chin
and elbow of the child.

ILLUSTRATION 6

Canvas shapes
Top—dramatic shapes
Bottom—static shapes

ILLUSTRATION 7

A watercolor drawing illustrates
the use of economy of
line to create the illusion of
a head. Sheer simplicity is
employed yet all three of the
basic line symbols have
been incorporated.

ILLUSTRATION 8

This gesture drawing was executed in a
matter of seconds with the use of continuous line.
The aim was to capture an attitude
of the model rather than an exact likeness.
Such technique can often be more
appealing than a factual drawing created
through laborious effort. The emotional impact
is strong because of the fluid flow of line.

ILLUSTRATION 9

This illustration, executed rapidly in chalk, emphasizes action
as well as attitude. Again the drawing was created
with a rapid continuous line. The employment of gesture drawing as a
self-teaching form is invaluable to the student.

ILLUSTRATION 10

This gesture drawing was created
with brush and ink on
Bristol board. The sketch was
executed rapidly, employing
all the line symbols. A
two tone wash was incorporated
into the drawing to add
weight and dimension.

ILLUSTRATION 11

This two part illustration is designed to aid you in identification of positive and negative space. The top diagram denotes a canvas shape before an imprint has been made. Because the shape is completely enclosed it is positive and represents the total available space. Some contemporary painters have exploited this phenomenon by painting a given surface one solid color thus taking advantage of this basic compositional principle. It cannot be denied that a canvas, before it receives the painter's first imprint, is a positive shape and is preferable over a poorly designed effort, yet it is far from a work of art.

The lower diagram denotes the placement of an object into the selected shape. Now the object shape is positive and the background is negative. Although the background shape is also enclosed by the periphery lines of the canvas, the space now acts as a housing for the object and demands an established relationship between the object and the periphery lines.

You must now bind the object of these lines by dissecting the surrounding shape. In other words, all available space must be converted to positive shape.

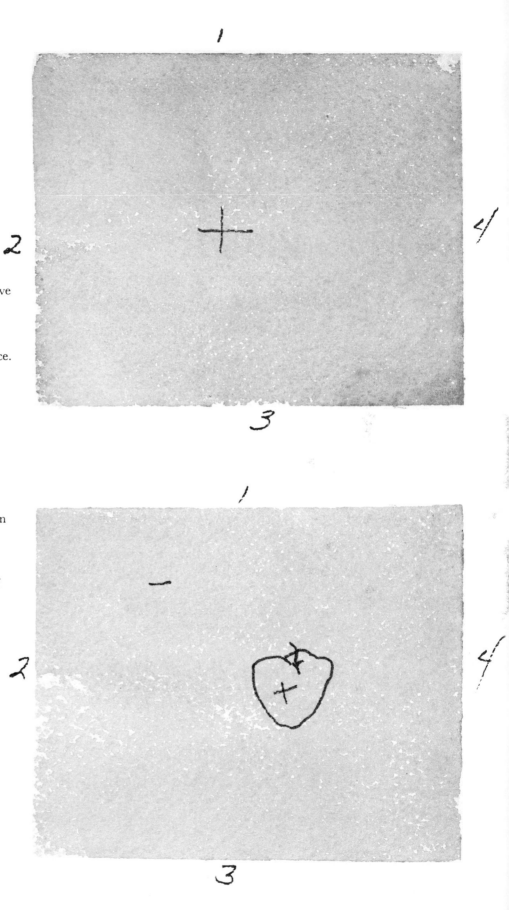

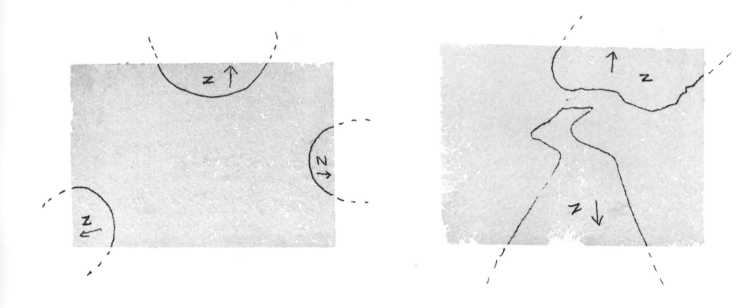

ILLUSTRATION 12

This two part illustration identifies the negative shapes
with the letter *N*. In the first example you will note the circular shapes
represent less than half of the total implied shape. The widest
part of the shape spreads along the periphery creating the illusion that
the major part of the suggested shape lies outside of the canvas.
Anytime a shape is designed in this manner the eye will
be forced out of the canvas at that point. The positive shape masses are
outside of the periphery line while the unidentifiable negative
area is inside the canvas border.
The second example illustrates the incorrect designing of a road or
stream with the widest section of the form placed along
the periphery line. The abstract mass encompassing the upper
right hand corner suggests a massive cloud shape. Both areas
are negative because they suggest that the positive shape rests outside of
the picture. The eye is pulled out of the picture plane
seeking the satisfying positive completion of the idea. More than
half the object must be inside of the canvas in order to create
an identifying illusion and to hold the space as positive space.
All important objects should be situated in the middle ground area
and held well away from periphery lines and corners.
Objects placed on the periphery or in the corners can upset
the balance of a painting. Such displacement of weight disrupts the axis
and rhythm you are attempting to establish. Success of such an idea
depends on pulling the funnel shape of the road back
into the painting and leading the eye in with structure lines.

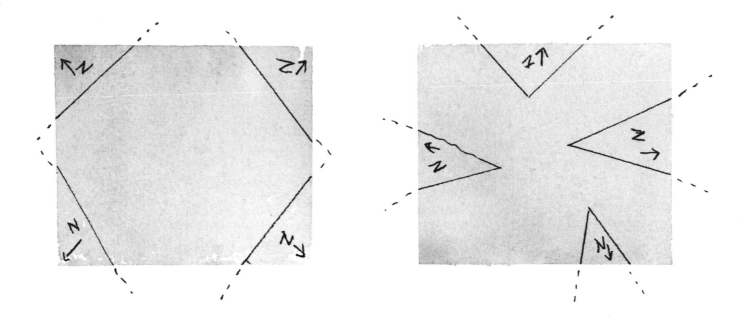

ILLUSTRATION 13

The first illustration portrays a common error.
The unsuspecting student, in an effort
to relieve the corners and keep them
unencumbered, will transform them into
triangles which are antagonistic to good order in
painting construction. The student should
neither weight the corners with unnecessary
paraphernalia nor leave them completely vacant.
Such treatment of corners can only
insure a poor design. The eye is drawn
to these unpleasant symmetrical shapes and
disturbed by this treatment.
The second diagram illustrates another
common pitfall. Again the symmetrical shapes
converge on the periphery lines causing the
eye to funnel out of the painting. All triangular
shapes are disagreeable forms unless
they can be manipulated and changed into
acceptable abstract positive shape.
The student should be continuously on
the alert for triangular shapes that can occur
inadvertently during a composition layout.

ILLUSTRATION 14

A more realistic example of negative
space is illustrated here. The top diagram
identifies the table and flowers as
positive shape. The background is floating. It is a
completely negative area unbound by
structure emphasis to the picture plane. The
shape is almost equal to the area consumed
by the positive shapes. This equalization of
positive and negative always tends to diminish
the positive and make it appear smaller
than it actually is. If negative areas
are deliberately designed into a composition
they must represent a small fraction of
the surface. The negative area must
be rehabilitated into positive shape by the
application of structure lines
and possibly additional objects.
The lower example is much more complicated.
Almost all of the area is designed in
negative space, even the table. The
background and the table line force the
eye out of the painting at the second, third and
fourth periphery lines. The objects
are enclosed and positive but they remain
unrelated to each other, causing negative shape
between the positive forms. The positive
shapes should be pulled together to form a total
positive area and the background
redesigned to be counted as positive shape.

ILLUSTRATION 15

Using the motif ideas in #14, I have illustrated
a solution to the negative shape problems.
The first diagram shows a broadening
of the floral motif, stretching it to encompass the
total space. The flower forms touch the
first, second and fourth periphery lines, tying
the motif to the outside structure.
The background has been broken into four
shapes instead of one continuous floating
area. The shapes now act as positive
areas because they are surrounded
by the enclosing forms of the flowers. The motif
is successfully housed in positive shape.
The lower illustration has been extended to
include a wall to the right and striped
wallpaper motif in the background. The table
was redesigned in a parallel structure
and the objects unified to form one massive
shape. All negative areas have been changed now
into positive shape. The composition
meets all the requirements of a
successful structure.

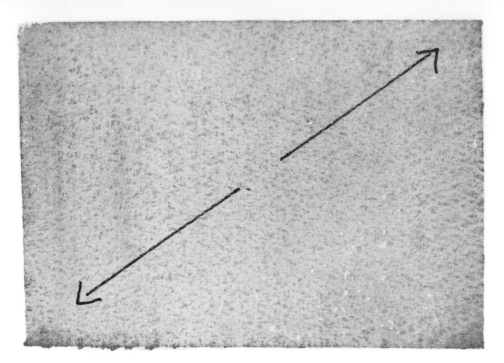

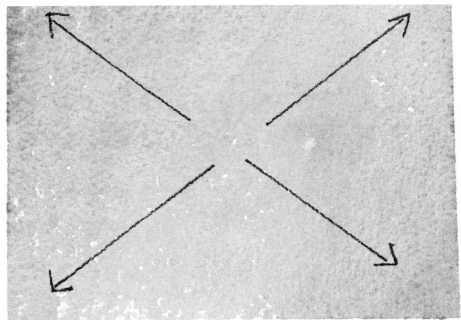

ILLUSTRATION 16

Negative shape can also result from the incorrect
use of directional lines within the motif
idea. For instance, a light pattern, a flower
stem or table edge, when directed to a
corner, can create a line emphasis that will
cause devastating division of the surface
into objectionable triangular shapes. This can
occur even if all the negative areas
have been concisely converted to positive shape.
A strong directional line can create enough
force to negate the positive shapes. All
too often a painting is designed allowing
the contour of the motif to form a directional
corner pull. The background area
forms a corner to corner triangular division.

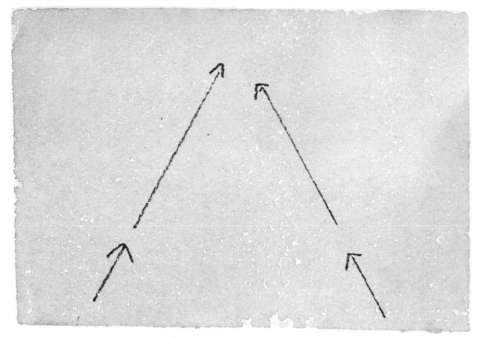

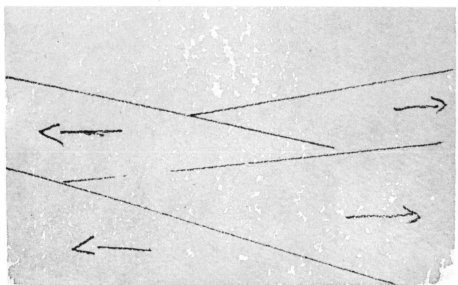

ILLUSTRATION 17

The top illustration denotes the directional
pull of a design built on the traditional
pyramid. Three triangular shapes of equal
strength are created. The eye will travel in an up
and down movement converging at
the points of the triangle instead of moving
rhythmically over the entire surface. The
completely symmetrical result is a static,
boring pattern.

The lower diagram denotes a design commonly
employed by the landscape painters.
It can only be successful if the painter is
aware of its pitfalls and can compensate
for its faults. The funnel shapes are stretched
diagonally through the canvas shape
and converge on the outside periphery
lines. The eye will be pulled
outside of the painting unless proper
preventive forces are introduced.

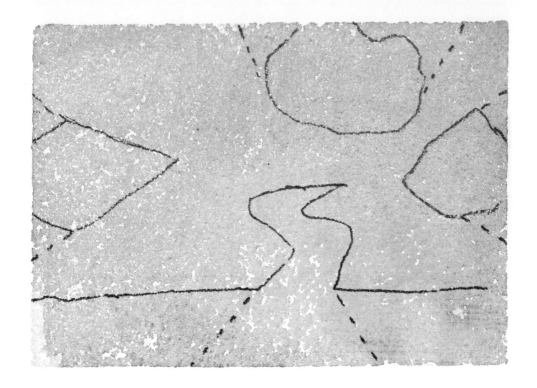

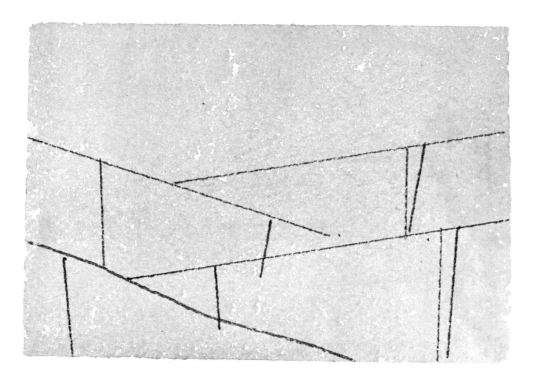

ILLUSTRATION 18

These two illustrations explain the
redesigning of circles, triangles and funnels
which were previously shown as negative shapes.
In the top diagram the circular shapes
have been readjusted to include the majority
of their shapes within the canvas.
The funnel shape of the road has been
pulled back into the picture and a
strong parallel plane has been added to hold the
eye into the inner surface.
The bottom diagram illustrates another
way of dealing with funnel shapes
by dissecting them with vertical lines and shapes
thus forcing the eye to remain within
the surface of the painting. Funnel shapes can
also be controlled through the use of a light
and dark tone variation and by
strong color control in the middleground
area of the painting.

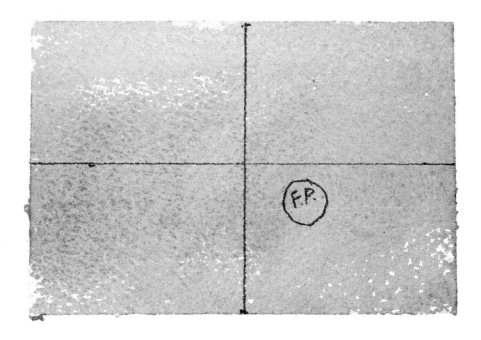

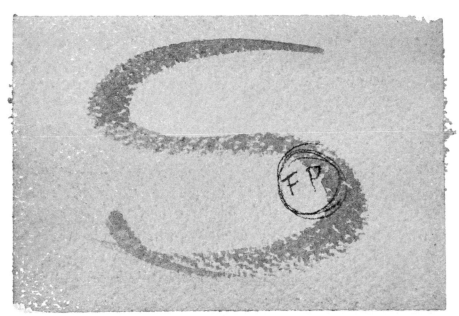

ILLUSTRATION 19

The first diagram illustrates the division of
the canvas into four parts with
the focal point placed in the lower right section.
This location on the canvas is the natural
choice to attract the eye and hold the
balance of the structure. It is unusual to find
the focal point located in another
area, and when it is, the care and planning of a
composition is much more difficult.
I would repeat here for purpose of emphasis
that the viewer's eye must enter the
painting at a determined point, travel the
surface, enjoy the experience and exit
the painting at the focal point area. The eye
must never be forced out of the painting
by negative areas or strong periphery color.
A successful painting will
hold the eye within its boundaries.
The term "point of interest" refers to the
dominant subject idea; it is never the focal point.
The eye is directed to the point of
interest by the rhythm which began at
the focal point. The focal point is always
incorporated within the surface rhythm
of the painting. To insure the flow of the eye,
the focal point color is repeated in an
understatement many times throughout the
selected rhythm pattern. The focal
point color is always the strongest color
on the painting surface.

ILLUSTRATION 20

CEZANNE PERSPECTIVE

The drawing is an analysis of Cezanne's special concept in composition.
He allows the viewer to see the objects at several eye levels
while convincing the viewer that the distortion of perspective is
correct. The three visible table areas are placed in positions
contrary to ordinary perspective presenting the viewer with three
different points of reference. The cloth separating the table
surface is amply designed to consume the majority of the table space
allowing the viewer to accept the variation of perspective.
Study the objects composing the still life and you will see that
the pitcher is viewed from a side perspective while the large jug is seen
from a higher vantage point. The basket is seen from
the side and is resting in space yet seems to be convincingly
setting on the table. Note that the pitcher and small jug
are tipped slightly to the left, upsetting the natural vertical axis,
causing a play of axial tensions between the various objects.
Cezanne's landscapes often are designed with the same pictorial illusion
of several points of view and tipped vertical axis. He gives
one the impression of reversing perspective by designing the shapes
in the foreground of the picture on a small scale
and enlarging the house shapes in the background.
The conflicting axis tensions, the presentation of many points
of view and the employment of reverse perspective are the
essence of Cezanne compositions.

3

Choosing a Theme

ACCEPTABLE SUBJECT MATTER

COMPOSITION IN PART is the harmonious arrangement of objects in a given space. These objects may be simply a shape or pattern, but if you, the student, wish to explore the pictorial subject, then you must conform to a standard of taste.

Taste is an illusive term and *standard* is even more so. Still, ignorance of the basic principles of taste can prevent a good talent from succeeding. Consequently, choice of subject matter must be controlled by rules to support the learning process of the student.

The selection of acceptable subject matter is often neglected by the teacher and consequently the student fails to learn the essence of good taste. The acquiring of taste is a learned experience. It is not innate with any painter. I have enumerated some subjects and categorized them under still life, landscape, head and figure subjects to aid the student in his learning process.

STILL LIFE SUBJECTS

Careful consideration must be given to the individual flower and its intrinsic design. Some flowers, although beautiful, simply do not have the necessary qualifications for a flower subject. For example, the exotic orchid is too intricate to be considered a suitable subject. The common garden variety of flower is a better choice. You are seeking simplicity of form and compact shape. The bouquet should appear casual. Tie a string about the stems and pop them into a container, allowing the blooms to fall where they may.

The container can determine the success or failure of a floral composition. The selection must be made with care and consideration for the role it will assume. The container should present a positive attitude or posture, expressing its ability to sustain the flowers in an upright position. If the space allotted to the vase is too small, it will fail to convince the viewer of its capacity to do the job. Because of this, *the vase should consume at least one third to one half of the space allotted to the flower motif.* Keep the vase simple and classic so it will not compete with the flowers. If the painter intends for the vase to be the dominant item of the composition, then the flowers must be held in the secondary position by reducing their size and color.

Avoid small, intricate containers, tiny mouthed vases and those with handles and flutes. Never use round bottomed containers without a base. They create a visual floating or rolling sensation, destroying the illusion that the subject is firmly seated upon a surface. *Preference must be given to the simple and unadorned.* Three basic shapes, the cylinder, the oval and the circle can be extended endlessly to form good containers to hold floral arrangements or as subjects by themselves.

Fruits and vegetables are acceptable as long as they are universal and not exotic and unusual. The accessory subjects such as table, chairs, clocks and books should be general in design and best if they do not carry the stamp of a certain period or culture. If you choose to work with a period design, you should be singular in your selection. Do not choose a hodge-podge of items from unrelated periods.

Never paint objects in fragments. More than half of any shape must be painted in order to explain the object. Avoid placement of one object directly above another. Have a plan, establish a rhythm by beginning with the focal point and moving to the point of interest, encompassing the total theme.

LANDSCAPE

The landscape motif is possibly the most difficult to assemble. The motif must be simplified and composed from a confounding vastness of subject matter. A camera can be useful to cut the complexity of the view. All trivia and miscellaneous material should be eliminated. Do not attempt to paint "on the spot". Amass drawings of the intended subject and once back in the studio, you can reassess the value of the idea with greater objectivity. This time element is an advantage to you: the creative process has had a period in which to function.

The landscape must have a single theme. Trees, rocks, water, sky, mountains, all relate to one another, but one single idea must emerge. Again, you must look for the universal language for your personal interpretation. You must avoid the spectacular, the flamboyant, the dramatic. I have in mind here, the sunset. Beautiful, yes, but too beautiful to carry validity in paint.

The typical amateur painter's landscapes rest as a blight upon the living rooms of our land. These amateurs across the country seem to gravitate to their regional landscape drama. The coast painters delight in depicting the surging, pounding waves striking the rocks of the coast line, sometimes adding a tree distorted by the elements to increase the drama of the scene. The midwesterners portray the chromatic array of their abundant foliage, hence the term "Buckeye Painters". Then there are the "Bluebonnet Painters" of Texas and the "Purple Mountain Painters" of New Mexico. Perhaps the most offensive I have observed are the landscape painters of the Northwest known as the "Teton Painters". When a bit of extra drama is needed (as if the Teton Mountain Range needed more) the bawling moose is portrayed majestically on the snowy slopes.

I mention this so you will not fall victim to your own sentimentality. A painter's role is not that of the camera or of a motion picture director. His is to perceive the beauty and rhythm of the landscape and express it through his eyes and talent as a personal experience.

THE HEAD

Choose a subject within your cultural experience. Identify with your model! Your attention should be directed to the attitude, the essence of the expression rather than the feature resemblance. *The facial planes must be in repose.* Never paint a smiling, toothy head. Such a portrait belongs to the photographer.

The model should be comfortably placed, relaxed. Do not dramatize the pose. Place the head so that the nose is held into the oval of the face. The use of the profile is questionable as to validity. The irregular contour of the features create movement which is disconcerting to the eye. A profile pose seems to be inherently a sculptural one and not a painter's cup of tea.

Place the model in a classic lighting position. That is, there must be a single source of light and that light must be from one side or the other. Think of the head in three-quarter view, turned from the light source. The front planes fall into shadow. Place the head in a full face position and the front planes are in middle tone. Turn the head to the three-quarter position into the light source and the front planes are in light. One other lighting situation can be used and that is to divide the head down the middle in either three-quarter or full position, resulting in one side of the head in light and one in shadow.

Avoid trappings on the head such as ribbons and bows, earrings and necklaces, hats and drapes. Keep the head simple and unadorned. The costume must play a minor role and be held in an understatement. Curved necklines are best because the round form is suited to the natural curve of the neck. Avoid intricate patterns such as lace or ruffles. Repeat: keep the costume simple.

The head should be concluded at the shoulders. Never cut the arms below the elbow and cause fragmentation of the motif. If you wish to paint more of the figure, the arms and hands must be included in the design. When your painting is planned to include more than one head, you must give one or the other the place of dominance. Never overlap one head with another. Such treatment usually destroys the form of both heads.

The head must be treated as a total statement. It will not be effectual if it is broken into fragments. This means that the *oval of the head must be maintained* without regard to the normal deviations such as the inset of the eyes, projection of the chin, or flow of the hair. Place the model in a position that will insure a continuity of contour line.

THE FIGURE

When speaking of the figure in composition, I am naturally assuming that the student has already acquired a topographical, anatomical knowledge of the structure of the human body. Without such knowledge the following notes will be of little value.

Convincing distortion is the essence of figure painting. The contemporary thought in the designing of the nude is the pear shape: a long, high-breasted upper torso with heavy buttox and legs. The shoulder is dropped and narrowed to facilitate the flow of contour line. The elbow will be in direct vertical position with the hipbone.

Keep the figure in a relaxed position no matter if it is standing, seated or reclining. Avoid contrived positions and attitudes of sexual connotation.

Do not fragment the figure. The three-quarter figure should be designed to include arms and hands. *Always indicate both hands.* Do not hide them under drapes or props to make your work easier. Cut the figure above the knee or continue the design to include the entire body. The balance of the figure is controlled by the hipbone as an axis with the mastoid and ankle bone in a plumb line.

Consider the beauty of the figure line. Design the figure by holding the arms and legs well into the torso. The total should be compact and solid without negative areas disrupting the contour flow.

Just as in the head, the light direction is simple and from one side of the figure. Such lighting insures simplicity and clarification of form.

Costumes must be simple, unencumbered with miscellaneous frills, buttons and laces. Keep it classic. Avoid the trivial styles of the day to eliminate dating the work. Patterned cloth can add a decorative quality but of secondary importance to the figure. If draping is used with the nude figure, do not allow it to appear contrived or cut into the body form, resulting in fragmentation. Use drapery only if it is necessary in the total rhythm and content of the composition.

Intriguing compositions can be developed by combining the figure with still life or landscape. The figure theme must be held intact with all other subject ideas relating harmoniously. Do not use period furniture as a decorative element. Props are designed only when necessary to explain the position of the model. The props, such as a table or chair cannot cut into the body design. This results in disruption of the design flow and fragmentation of the figure.

THE CHILD'S FIGURE

The child's figure must be given individual consideration. The subject is automatically sentimental. Consequently, exacting discipline must be enforced when considering the child as a painting theme.

The child's figure is designed in the pear shape: narrow neck and shoulders with the lower torso carrying the weight of the figure. The size of the neck and shoulders will identify the age level of the child. The legs should be short and full. The distortion of the arm length is not effective in the child's figure. To lengthen the upper arm so that the elbow rests at the hipbone level (as in the adult figure) tends to make the child seem all arm.

Design the limbs to flow with the torso of the figure: arms pulled to the side and legs together in a static position. Do not portray the child in the act of moving. Such portrayal increases the sentimentality of the image and places it in the category of illustration. Choose simple costumes and simple surroundings and play down the drama of the situation.

If props are used, the choice should be classic. For example, a rag doll is preferable over a modern life-like plastic replica. The attitude of the doll should be disjointed, stuffed and toy-like, and be completely held in an understatement. Do not use props unless they are necessary for the harmony of the theme.

COMPARATIVE ANALYSIS
OF ILLUSTRATION VERSUS FINE ART

It is imperative that we differentiate between Illustrative and Fine Art. This may be a new thought for some students. A confusion of standard of Fine Art and Illustrative Art is extremely common. The illustrator attempts to characterize man and his surroundings. The fine artist attempts to capture universal truth and beauty.

CHARACTERIZATION VERSUS CLASSIC BEAUTY

The illustrator adheres to duplication of the physical appearance of his subject. The connotation of characterization is exaggeration of individual characteristics. The illustrator will emphasize the peculiarities of his subject rather than seeking the basic beauty of the human form.

The fine artist must relate with his model if he expects to express the essence of the subject. Consequently, he would never alienate himself by selecting a model outside of his own culture.

COMPLEXITY VERSUS SIMPLICITY

The illustrator frequently employs a multiplicity of subjects to convey his pictorial idea. Complication and overstatement often occur.

The fine artist limits himself to *one subject only*. All extraneous material is eliminated. All objects in a motif must be necessary to portray the theme. A figure painting may contain many figures as long as each one denotes a single idea. Cezanne's "Bathers", for example, is composed of several figures and all are involved in bathing. Consequently, there is only one subject idea.

REGIONAL VERSUS UNIVERSAL

The rustic covered bridges of New England, the tobacco sheds of the Southeast, and the potato houses of the Northwest are all illustrative subjects of their peculiar surroundings and needs of the communities. They are purely colloquial and are not communicative to a general audience. No matter how appealing and nostalgic these subjects are, the fine artist must refrain from the urge to paint them. His topic must carry a universal communication not only for his time but hopefully for future generations.

SENTIMENTAL VERSUS UNEMOTIONAL

The illustrator employs sentimentality as an instrument of general appeal. Sentimentality implies affectations and plays on the nostalgic remembrances, accounting for its general popularity with the average audience. Fine art is an expression of the passive voice and can be understood by the study of the masterpieces of the past. The fine artist cannot allow himself to be influenced by sentiment. This does not mean that the painter himself is devoid of emotion. On the contrary, the painter must employ great empathy and deeply perceive the essence of his subject.

ACTIVE VERSUS STATIC

The illustrator records children at play, racing horses, moving trains, people in the midst of all types of activity and great events of history, acting upon the drama of the moment for his statement.

The language of the fine artist is one of repose, tranquility and serenity. He is more apt to catch a figure in a relaxed, natural position, seeking beauty of design rather than to record a story.

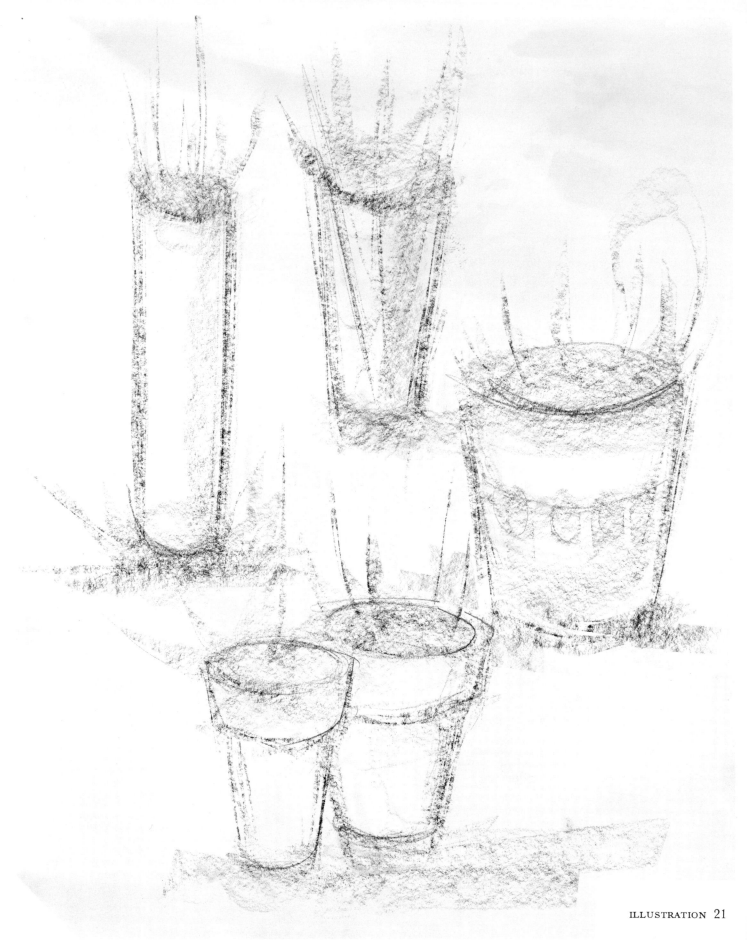

ILLUSTRATION 21

Cylinder shapes

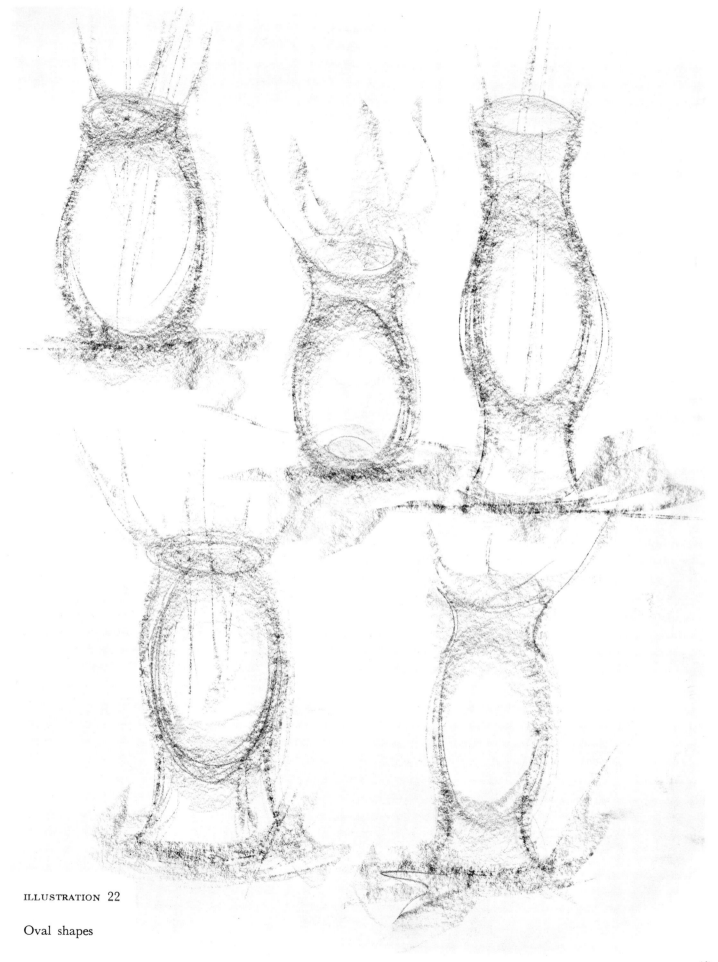

ILLUSTRATION 22

Oval shapes

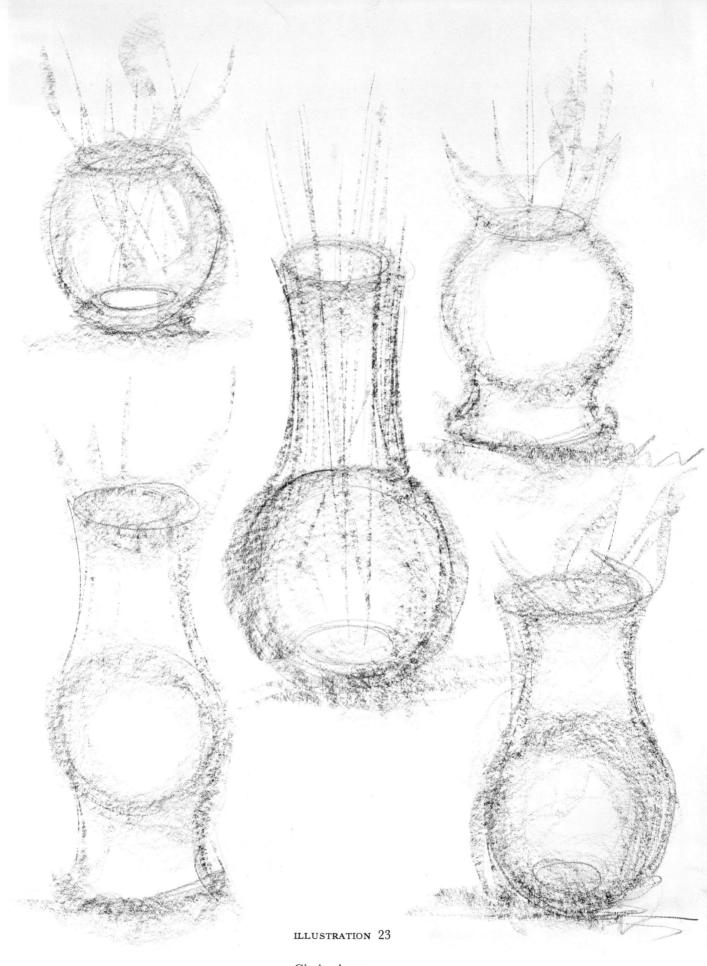

ILLUSTRATION 23

Circle shapes

ILLUSTRATION 24

Front facial planes in shadow

ILLUSTRATION 25

Front facial planes in middle tone

ILLUSTRATION 26

Front facial planes in light

ILLUSTRATION 27

Light and shade divided by the central axis line

ILLUSTRATION 28

These two heads have been
designed to complement each
other, yet each head is a
complete statement. The facial
ovals and neck cylinders
remain unencumbered. A space
has been placed between the
heads to allow for the separation
of contour lines. The hair
areas are unified to insure the
continuous line flow.

ILLUSTRATION 29

When painting the boy or adult
male, position the head so
that the ear is inside of the
back of the oval. Do not allow
the ears to protrude and
disturb the flow of the
contour line; rather, seek a unity
of the ear to prevent forming
a pocket of negative shape.
The hair should be long enough
to meet the form of the ear
without interruption.

CORRECT

INCORRECT

ILLUSTRATION 30

The hair should be simply dressed and held well away from
the face and neck. The hair contour line must never interfere with the
head oval and neck cylinder. When this occurs the oval
and cylinder become flat nondescript shapes and the illusion of a
curved surface is lost.

55

ILLUSTRATION 31

The head diagrams illustrate the age of the
individual by the placement of the eye
axis line and by establishing the
proper relationship of the neck and shoulders
to the head oval.

From the years 1-12 the eyes are in the center of
the head. The eyes begin to move up in
the facial oval during puberty. When
the child has reached maturity the eyes will
be above center.

The neck of an infant from 1 to 5 is narrow and
short. The shoulders are drawn only
slightly wider than the width of the head.

The next diagram shows the neck
slightly longer but the shoulders kept narrow.
Any place between the ages of 10 and
the early 20's, you can observe astonishing
changes in the eye and neck development. The
eyes move continuously higher in the
facial oval and the nose usually elongates.
The neck becomes longer and in the
male, much thicker. For design purposes, the
neck is always drawn longer than it
actually appears to be and the shoulders
are sloped—even in the male.

In the fourth diagram you see a female
adult with the eyes high in the head and the
neck elongated. The
shoulders are narrow and sloped.

The adult male appears the same except for
the thickness of the neck and a wider shoulder.

The last diagram denotes old age.
The facial oval sags and the neck
becomes short and wide in both the
female and the male.

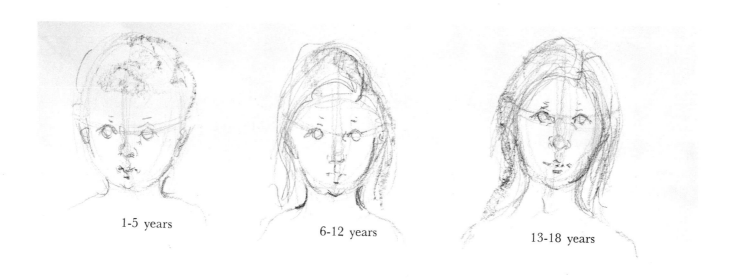

1-5 years   6-12 years   13-18 years

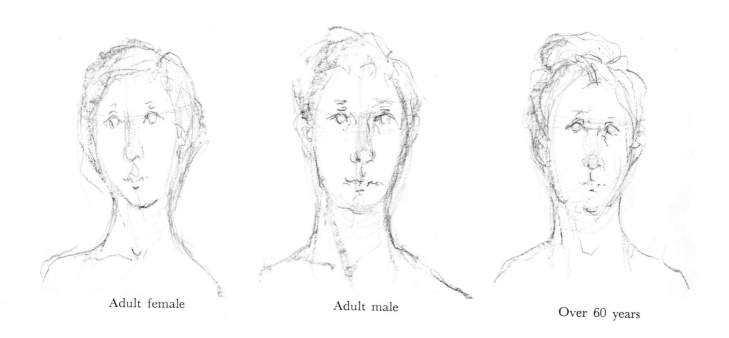

Adult female   Adult male   Over 60 years

ILLUSTRATION 32

The arrows on the right side
of the illustration denote
the correct places to cut the
figure. Any other selection (such
as below the elbow or the
knee) results in fragmentation.
Note also that the light
source for the drawing is
from the left, exposing the front
facial and body planes
in light and the side planes
in shadow. If the light source
had been directed from
the right, the front planes would
fall into shadow. If the figure
had been turned full front,
the light from either side would
have thrown the front planes
into middle tone.
The illustration also
demonstrates the figure in
repose, the arms held into the
body and adorned in a
simple classic costume.

4

Application of the Principles of Composition

EXPERIMENTS

1. STRAIGHT LINE SYMBOLS
2. STRAIGHT LINE SYMBOLS IN COMBINATION
3. CURVED LINE SYMBOLS
4. STRAIGHT LINE SYMBOLS WITH MOTIF

Materials:

Tracing paper

Newsprint

Vine charcoal or pastel chalk

IDENTIFICATION OF STRUCTURE

THIS SECTION IS DEVOTED to a new concept of application to the structure in composition. You will now begin to apply the principles of composition. By studying the illustration, you can gain an immediate insight into the procedure. I would recommend a serious involvement if you are to gain the utmost value from the experiments. Once your imagination has been stimulated, you will be able to extend these patterns into many more intriguing structures.

My first experiment with the student and a compositional course of study began with the letters of the alphabet. The student was to stretch a single letter to the outer limits on the surface, adding other letters to supplement the main one until the plane was filled, with equal space allotted to light and dark pattern. The symbols utilized in this abstract concept have proved to be an automatic communication between teacher and student. The result was an understandable instrument that demonstrates the structure principle of composition. The light and dark patterns created by the combination of the straight line letters formed the foundation on which the student could build his composition.

The starting point of a painting is a theme, the inspiration of an idea. A painter must gather this theme together, eliminate all extraneous material, make a decision as to the medium in which he will work and then go about building a form to house his idea. This form is an abstract structure. It must consume the total surface. The structure is identified by the pattern of light and shade dispersed upon the allotted space. This is the scaffolding, the skeleton that supports the subject.

During this process of learning, you should allow the structure to precede the subject idea until the craft of constructing a structure is well in hand. It is best if you can divorce yourself from a pictorial theme. *Disintegration of structure* invariably occurs when a theme is introduced unless your mind is firmly committed to the structural idea. The straight line letters, *X, Y, T, H, I, L,* and *O* (built on the right angle rather than the circle, □), are all strong structural letters and can be combined to create endless imaginative abstract patterns.

Not all of the letters of the alphabet are practical symbols for adaptation as a structure. The letters formed by a combination of straight and curved lines, such as P, R, or B, create an ambiguity of line. Symmetrical letters, such as A, M, W, N or V, break the surface into pyramids and are not feasible structural concepts.

The curved line symbols: *S* or *C* are considered only in supplement to the straight line letter, the *S* being the more valuable. These are the rhythm letters and when utilized with color, will move the eye from point to point over the surface. The *S* symbol has long been accepted as a sound compositional theory but its presentation as a total compositional idea is a faulty concept. The *S* is valuable only as a surface treatment: a rhythm created to carry the eye over the surface. This rhythm symbol has been mistaken for a total structure idea because of its easily identifiable pattern on the surface of a painting. *It does not function as a structure.* It cannot be stretched effectively through the total space to the periphery lines. It is always contained in the center area of the painting. The *S* symbol does not bind or hold any object in space.

The fact that the *S* letter can encompass the focal point area makes it extremely useful in controlling the flow of the eye over the painting. When the curved letters are used with this basic principle in mind, they can be extremely valuable in developing the rhythm of a composition.

EXPERIMENTING WITH STRAIGHT LINE SYMBOLS

The diagrams that follow explain a few structure possibilities utilizing the straight line symbols and their adaptability to motif ideas. As you experiment with these letter symbols, keep in mind that one letter must dominate all others in a single structure idea. Any letters which are added to support or diversify the original letter must be held in subjugation to the main letter. If you choose to place a letter in a diagonal position into the canvas shape, the supplementary letters must be positioned predominantly diagonal. This insures a single thrust emphasis in the structure and prevents equalization of the parallel and diagonal movement.

The light and shade should be dispersed almost equally on the surface to insure the establishment of adequate contrast and identification of the structure.

Extend the letters into as many ideas as you possibly can by changing the shape of the canvas. The letters should be distorted; that is, the thickness and position of the letter lines should vary to the degree that they lose their identity as letter symbols. This will create a more intriguing and applicable abstract pattern to support a subject idea. Use the flat side of the chalk so that the letter forms a shape and not a line. The shape must be thick and irregular. Seek variation of tone by changing your pressure on the chalk.

A letter must never be placed to cut into a corner. Such treatment causes equal pyramiding of the shapes. When *triangles* are formed in the background area, supporting lines must be added to bisect the shapes and hold them inside of the picture plane. All shapes created by the letter symbols in the canvas must be positive.

EXPERIMENTING WITH
STRAIGHT LINE SYMBOLS IN COMBINATION

A single letter can be the total structural foundation but, by combining the straight line letters, endless ideas will germinate. The following diagrams are devised with one major letter dominating the surface. Other letters have been added to gain variation of structural ideas.

EXPERIMENTING WITH CURVED LINE SYMBOLS

The following diagrams are intended to show the adaptation of rhythm to the structure. The straight line symbols have been eliminated. You are concerned with moving the *S* and *C* within the canvas shape to control the surface eye movement. The focal point is placed within the curved pattern to facilitate the entrance and exit of the eye. An organized procedure such as this reduces the possibility of your falling into common design errors. You are concerned here only with the placement of objects in a given area and seeking harmonious relationships of shapes by balancing them on the curved letter symbols.

Remember, the straight line symbols reach to the edge of the surface and break the total surface into various shapes of light and dark pattern. The surface rhythm letters appear in the canvas center as a supplement to the dominant straight letter symbol. The curved letters are always involved with the focal point and are guide lines for the eye. The theme and rhythm patterns are superimposed over the structure and adapted to conform to the light and dark patterns.

Keeping all of these principles in mind, compose many complete ideas by utilizing several variations of the curved symbols. Be conscious of your experiments in symbolism, balancing your line movements and seeking variation of emotional emphasis. Check your surface for any negative shapes that may have been formed and correct them by holding them into the picture plane with contour line.

EXPERIMENTING WITH
STRAIGHT LINE SYMBOLS WITH MOTIF

Experiment with all of the letters in combination, allowing your thinking to encompass pictorial ideas. Draw your motifs on a sheet of thin transfer paper and lay them over structure patterns.

When you add a theme to a structure, you must maintain the dark and light structure pattern no matter where the motif falls. *Do not allow the structure to disintegrate.* Remember, a good structure will carry any pictorial idea. Reverse the light and dark structural pattern you have achieved and place the same drawings over the structure. The impact of the total effect changes completely.

A cartoon of a subject has been overlaid on some of the diagrams to show the correlation of theme with the structural idea. The completed painting follows these diagrams.

ILLUSTRATION 33

SINGLE DIAGONAL X

The first structure pattern is designed by
stretching a single X diagonally through an
almost square canvas shape. The X
strikes the four periphery lines at varying
positions forming different shapes in the light
background. The resulting pattern created
by the X fulfills all the requirements of a sound
structure. The light and dark areas
are equally dispersed. The design is abstract
and pleasing and will successfully house
a multitude of motif ideas.
The lower pattern is a reversal of the first,
utilizing the light X over a dark background.
This structure is equally as fine as
the first if you follow sound structural procedure.
The X must never be designed to strike
into the corners. Such division creates
objectionable triangles. It is also important
to realize that a structure design
should either strike diagonally across the picture
plane or parallel the periphery edge of
the canvas. It is even more imperative
to understand that a sound structure is never
conceived with both. If diagonal
and parallel structure lines are designed in
the same composition *with equal force*,
the emphasis becomes divided and the structure
is weakened. This does not mean
that a diagonal structure cannot house a few
parallel lines, but such additions should be
held in subjection to the main diagonal thrusts.

ILLUSTRATION 34

SINGLE DIAGONAL X

In the top example you are looking at a vertical
shaped canvas structured with a single
dark X which has been placed off center.
Again the pattern forms an almost
equalization of the light and dark and pulls to
all four periphery lines. The emotional
emphasis of this illustration has a tremendous
dramatic effect due to the change of canvas shape.
In the lower example, the canvas is placed
horizontally and the emotional pitch
becomes less dramatic and more serene.
Both are excellent structure designs and can be
adopted for numerous motif ideas.
When you are utilizing the single X be
sure that the lines do not converge
in the corners. Also, remember to keep one
dominant theme—diagonal or parallel—
when adding other lines to the structure. Both of
these illustrations can be turned to a
vertical or horizontal position, and
the light and dark areas can be reversed
to gain new structure patterns.

ILLUSTRATION 35

SINGLE PARALLEL X

The *X* is now placed in a horizontal canvas
shape and stretched through the total surface in
a parallel position. The emotional
emphasis now changes to a less dramatic
and more rigid expression. In the upper
diagram the *X* is placed off center, creating
a more varied background pattern.
All the resulting shapes are bound to the
periphery edge by the parallel
lines and are expressing solid, positive shape. The
canvas can be placed just as successfully in
any of the three remaining positions
to gain additional structure ideas.

The lower pattern illustrates a light *X* balanced
in the center of the horizontal canvas.
Contrary to what you may have been taught,
the equalization of shape does not preclude
a poor compositional idea. It simply
means the resulting emotional impetus is static.
Interesting compositional ideas
can be developed from this deliberate
monotonous shape relation.
The *X* is just as useful in a parallel pattern
as it is in a diagonal one. You must
maintain the parallel expression throughout
the design and hold to the almost equal
light and dark dispersion. You can experiment
with the *X* by changing its directional
emphasis, reversing light and
shade, and utilizing different canvas shapes.

ILLUSTRATION 36

SINGLE DIAGONAL Y

The *Y* is an automatic diagonal structure and
is always successful when it is properly
distorted and designed with the canvas shape and
motif in mind. The lines of the *Y*
must never be allowed to cut into a corner
or form triangles.
Here you see the dark and light *Y* stretching
through the total canvas shape in a
diagonal sweep but touching only the first,
second, and fourth periphery lines. The
background shapes are negative because they
flare at the periphery lines. Some
adjustment must be made to draw these
shapes back into the surface. This can be

managed by adding diagonal structure
lines to break up the negative areas and turn
them positive. You can also manipulate the
areas with color variations and textural emphasis
to control the negative shapes.
This *Y* pattern is adaptable in any position.
Experiment with the *Y* by changing the
canvas shape. Distorting the *Y* by changing the
angles of the line is another method with
which to experiment. When the *Y* symbol is
distorted greatly and a parallel right
angled design is created, the *Y* obviously becomes
a *T*. The *T* is discussed thoroughly
in following diagrams. The *Y* is extremely
adaptable to a landscape motif. I have
also seen it used with great success when
incorporated with a floral or street scene subject.

ILLUSTRATION 37

SINGLE DIAGONAL Y

These patterns were designed with the *Y* in a vertical position in an almost square canvas shape. The emotional impact is still quite dramatic because the *Y* is upright and encounters two periphery lines. The second and fourth periphery lines are free of contact. The resulting background shapes are again negative. There is a small triangle formed at the top of the design which needs to be rehabilitated into positive space. All of these areas require additional diagonal lines, color or texture to keep them moving inside of the picture plane.

In the lower illustration the *Y* has been deliberately distorted. The width of the symbol changes as it moves over the surface. The contour lines are also held loosely, compensating for the once triangular shape formed by the converging of the upper structure of the letter. Additional diagonal emphasis will have to be designed into the pattern to break up the large dark masses on either side of the *Y*. These patterns should be turned in vertical positions to gain additional structure patterns. Again, these patterns are extremely versatile and adaptable to both landscape and still life motifs.

ILLUSTRATION 38

SINGLE DIAGONAL Y

Again we are looking at a pattern
created by the versatile Y, this time in horizontal
position. The Y is stretched only to the first,
second and third periphery lines.
In both examples the background space exceeds
the letter space, meaning that the top
pattern is dominated by light and the lower
is predominantly dark. There is not
an equalization of tone values present,
but it is close enough to be effective.

When these patterns are turned into a vertical
position the emotional thrusts change into a
more powerful effect. Experiment
with the Y in various shapes and positions.
A multitude of Y structures are available
to you. Distort the Y by changing the width of
the symbol and by positioning it in
different angles through the canvas shape.
Remember that additional structure lines
prompted by the adaptation of a motif must be
incorporated in the same diagonal
emphasis so that the initial attitude of
the Y can be maintained.

ILLUSTRATION 39

SINGLE PARALLEL T

The *T* actually carries the same basic structure
as the *Y,* but now you are seeing it in a
parallel, right angled pattern. The emotional
effect is more formal and rigid than
in the *Y* structure. To utilize the *T* correctly, you
must be aware of the evenly designed shapes
and use them to your advantage
by adapting a motif to coincide with the
already marked formal emphasis. Any
additional lines that are used during the
application of the subject idea
should be predominantly parallel and
placed at right angles to the existing
pattern and the periphery lines of the canvas.
When the canvas shapes are placed in a
vertical position the projected image is drastically
transformed. It no longer identifies
strongly with a figure or still life motif but is
reminiscent of building forms such as
windows and doors. When the patterns are
completely turned around into the
opposite horizontal positions, street scenes can be
adapted successfully to the structure.

ILLUSTRATION 40

SINGLE PARALLEL T

Here you are seeing the paralleling T placed
into long narrow shapes. The top pattern carries
strong dramatic emphasis. It is extremely
adaptable to still life, florals and
figure painting. The number one periphery
line is free of the T symbol and actually
is bound to a light I. Because of its
parallel placement, the shape holds tightly to the
canvas edge. The surface is totally positive
and can be used successfully
without additional structure lines.
The lower illustration explains a light T
in a long horizontal shape and immediately
conveys a traditional landscape idea.
Again you see an I symbol which can be related
to sky while the light T represents fields
and tree areas. Any structure lines
that are superimposed by a landscape motif
should be held in parallel patterns to emphasize
the formal dispersion of light and shade.
The light T is placed off center. The point of
contact of the two lines of the T symbol is
located at the preferred focal point area, making
it very easy to correlate the movement
of the surface rhythm with the structure.
This pattern works equally well even
when it is inverted. Change the position of both
patterns and the whole structural emphasis
changes and implies a change in motif adaptation.

ILLUSTRATION 41

SINGLE PARALLEL H

The *H* is extremely versatile in its structural possibilities due to the presence of another structure line in the symbol. Here you are seeing the bars of the *H* placed parallel to each other and to the periphery edge. The background shapes are increased in number and in shape variation. Still, the patterns are near equalization in the dispersement of light and dark areas.

The emotional attitude of both illustrations is strict and rigid. Turn the pattern to a vertical position and it will assume a more forceful attitude. The design can no longer be easily recognized as an *H*. The letter symbols should always be distorted to the extent that they operate as abstract structural patterns and not as identifiable letters. Your own experiments in distortion and placement of the symbols will enlighten you as to their great versatility. Experiment also with various shapes in both horizontal and vertical positions and note the extreme variety of emotional emphasis that can be achieved. Reverse light and shade and change the positioning of the symbols in the canvas shapes.

71

ILLUSTRATION 42

SINGLE DIAGONAL H

The *H* is now placed diagonally in the surface encountering the right angles of the rectangular canvas shape. The dramatic force is increased by this positioning and lends a certain excitement to the effect.
The background patterns are varied and predominantly positive in feeling. Any diagonal pattern will create some problems in negative space. Lines added to rehabilitate the shapes should never disrupt the diagonal thrust of the patterns.

When the canvas shapes are turned to a vertical position the *H* again loses its identity as a letter and acts as abstract form. Experiment with the two horizontal structure lines of the *H* in this position by changing the angles. The emotional emphasis will vary according to the positioning of the bars. Experiment with various canvas shapes and distort the width and contour of the symbol.
The *H* has tremendous possibilities in adaptation to motif ideas. It seems to be equally effective in still life, landscape and figure motifs. The *H* is often recognizable as structure under Goya's paintings.

ILLUSTRATION 43

SINGLE PARALLEL I

This illustration is possibly the simplest of
structural ideas: the division of a
surface, more or less down the middle, forming
a simple light and dark dispersement.
When the *I* is used in this manner it must
always parallel the periphery lines in order
to hold the balance of the structure.
The *I* has been utilized through the ages in head
and figure painting. Its success is greatly
due to the use of classical lighting to identify the
form of the head and figure. When it
goes astray it is due to a faulty concept
of lighting. The unschooled painter will reverse
the background light and shade,
believing that such a reversal will emphasize
the dramatic quality of the painting.
Actually he is confusing the light source by
such treatment. *The light side of the
figure should always correspond to the light side
of the background.*
Turn the pattern to a horizontal position
and you will see the traditional
landscape pattern. Additional paralleling *I*
symbols can be incorporated to move
the emphasis from the center of the canvas.
Endless variations of the *I* composition can be
adapted. The *S* symbol can be successfully
superimposed over the structure lines
to gain perspective in the landscape and to insure
rhythmical eye movement over the
surface. In this position the earth area is
dark and the sky light. Reverse the positions
and a striking change of mood
is introduced into the landscape motif.

ILLUSTRATION 44

SINGLE PARALLEL L

The *L* is another traditional structure. Edgar
Degas exploited its structural importance both as
a parallel and as a diagonal structure.
"The Mante Family" by Degas is an
example of the *L* in parallel. You can easily
identify a dark *L* pattern in the upper half
of the canvas. It is supported by a light
square at the upper left and a dark
square in the lower half: very simply and tightly
structured. The three figures are superimposed
over the structural foundation. Degas also
utilized the *L* in diagonal compositions
with great success. It should be kept in mind that
the diagonal *L* will create triangles which
must be destroyed by dissection of the shapes.

The *L* is extremely well suited for
interior designs because of its simplicity
and its strong, solid appearance. Street
scenes can be adapted with ease to the *L*
structure. The canvas can be turned in various
positions and the resulting change of
emphasis is equally adaptable to structural motifs.
You should experiment with this single
letter in different shapes and positions. The
background shapes formed by the *L*
vary from rectangular shapes to the square.
You can disrupt the contour lines
of the letter by widening and narrowing
the *L* symbol at different points and
gain a multitude of fluctuating light effects.
The light and dark dispersion
should be held almost equal and parallel
or diagonal emphasis maintained.

ILLUSTRATION 45

SINGLE PARALLEL O (□)

The first illustration denotes the placement
of a right angled (square) *O* in an almost
static surface. The composition lacks the
dramatic structure form but it still can be
extremely useful to the painter.
This idea of chiaroscuro was exploited by
Rembrandt. His canvases often were
predominantly dark. The light was dramatically
focused on the facial planes of the portrait
or directed to the important figure
arrangement. It would behoove the serious
student to study the dispersion of light
and shade employed by this master. Look for the
light *H, T, O* and *L* forms he used
repeatedly. His etchings and drawings are
perhaps even more enlightening than
his paintings when approaching a structural study.
Control of the *O* as a lighting device can
give the painter a tremendous advantage in
exploiting abstracted light over a motif:
meaning, no matter where the motif falls the
light pattern would dominate the
surface and control the mood and style of
work. Any structural pattern can be
employed and the light *O* superimposed
over it as the dominant letter.
The lower illustration can be recognized as a
legitimate structure form of the watercolor
painter. The motif is held dominantly
in center stage with the light *O* forming a
frame of white around the painting. A structural
pattern such as this is more suited to the
graphic and watercolor media than to oil painting.

ILLUSTRATION 46

SINGLE PARALLEL O (□)

This illustration presents a concept of
identifying the *O* in rectangles and squares.
The patterns are absolutely positive and
strongly bound to the surface by the parallel
lines, utilizing the total available space.
In the top horizontally placed shape,
the dispersion of light and dark is extremely
adaptable to portrait and figure work just
as is the *I*. The head or figure motif
can be superimposed over the pattern and the
light side of the head or figure corresponds
to the light of the structure.
The bottom pattern explains the structure
in a narrow vertical shape. Here you see an
automatic landscape structure. The patterns are
extremely versatile in their application
to interior structures and street scenes.
The square and the rectangle are
natural partners, one complementing the other.
The evidence of utilization of this
structure idea is present in all periods of art.
A painter may not have structured
deliberately with the square and rectangle
in mind, yet, by analyzing works of the
past and present, the rectangle
and square can be identified in abundance.

ILLUSTRATION 47

DOUBLE PARALLEL X

Your experiments will now expand into
structural patterns employing double letters in
combination. The first is a design
developed by the use of two *X* symbols stretched
through the surface in a parallel pattern.
You will note that one *X* dominates
the surface. It is well to remember that one
letter should carry the greater impact.
The resulting pattern now begins to lose
its identity as letter symbols and operate as pure
abstract pattern. Experiment with
these two like symbols by reversing the light
and shade pattern and by changing the
relationship of the letters to each other and to
the canvas surface. Apply distortion to the
forms by fluctuating the contour line
and by increasing and decreasing the width
of the symbols. Keep the light and dark
almost equally dispersed and maintain the formal
attitude of the parallels. Do not add
structural emphasis that will conflict with
the parallel structure. Experiment with
various canvas shapes in vertical
and horizontal positions.
This structural pattern is extremely suitable
to endless still life and landscape motifs.
The objects can be arranged
over the structure in an almost haphazard
manner. An *S* rhythm can be superimposed to
control eye movement. The dark structure
will tie the object together if the light and shade
of the structure is maintained. *Do not
allow disintegration of the light
and shade pattern of the structure!*

ILLUSTRATION 48

DOUBLE DIAGONAL Y

Two light *Y* symbols are combined to create
this pleasing abstract pattern. The letters
now lose their identity as letters. There are some
negative shapes created in the dark
background which must be broken and
changed either by adding diagonal
structure lines or by varying the color values
or employing textural emphasis.
The patterns which result from the combining
of these like symbols can be endlessly
extended by changing the positioning of

the letters, reversing the light and dark
and by placing them in different shaped surfaces.
The structure is especially adaptable
to nonobjective and abstract style of painting,
yet a realistic still life motif could be united
with the structure effectively.
A landscape could be superimposed by
adapting the land area to the *Y* in the
lower half of the surface and creating a sky
pattern with the *Y* at the top.
When the design is turned to a vertical
position it suggests rough mountain
terrain. An *S* rhythm symbol can be superimposed
over the lower half of the structure to control
eye movement and perspective.

ILLUSTRATION 49

DOUBLE PARALLEL T

In this illustration the larger of the *T* symbols
is set in an upside down position with
the smaller *T* in an upright attitude. The
shapes created in the structure are completely
positive and tightly bound to the canvas
edge. The light and dark dispersion
is almost equal. The shape can be turned to
its horizontal positions and the emotional
emphasis changes immediately.
The pattern is adaptable to a double
floral idea or a multiple still life arrangement.

Also, street scenes, interiors and structural
ideas are extremely successful on this pattern
because of the parallel emphasis.
Experiment with the dual *T* structure by
changing the relationship of the letters
and distorting the width of the symbols. The
shape can be elongated in either the
horizontal or vertical position and increase
the number of structural ideas.
Remember that any additional structural lines
which are included in the rendering of
a motif must be predominantly in parallel
accents. The right angled pattern
must remain the dominant force in the structure.

ILLUSTRATION 50

DOUBLE DIAGONAL H

This illustration demonstrates a structural
idea involving the converging of two *H* symbols
in a diagonal position on a vertical
surface. You will note that the identity
of the letters has been lost. The
pattern is seen now as an abstract pattern
due to the distortion of the letter forms
and the converging and overlapping of the letters.
The light and shade dispersement is
almost equal and all shapes are positive.
Experiment with the versatile *H* by
changing positions of the letters in both diagonal
and parallel situations. Do not combine
the two. Adapt the *H* symbols
to different shaped canvases and reverse the
light and shade patterns.
Structures created through the application
of the dual *H* are extremely suitable
to structural motifs such as street scenes and
interiors. The landscape opportunities are
numerous. The *S* rhythm symbol can be
incorporated into the motif and superimposed
over the structure to aid in
surface movement and perspective.
Still life and floral motifs can be superimposed
over this strong structure and held
together by the light and dark underlying
pattern. Figures can also be overlaid
and held into the structure by conscious
utilization of the structure force.

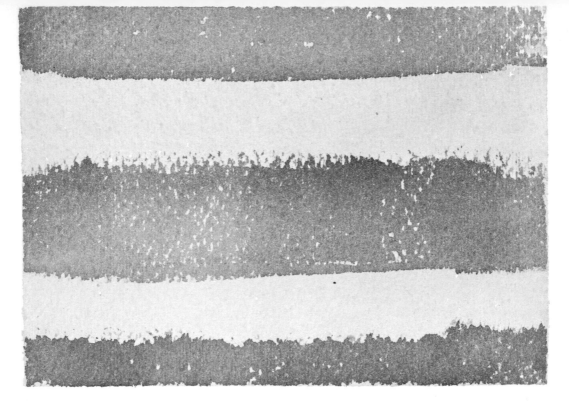

ILLUSTRATION 51

MULTIPLE PARALLEL I

This two part illustration depicts the use of multiple *I* symbols. The first example is a simple parallel structure which can be effective in either a horizontal or vertical position.

The lower illustration is a pattern created by positioning *I* symbols at right angles.

Both patterns are totally positive and extremely valuable structure ideas. Endless patterns can result from the combining of multiple *I* symbols. Experiment with the symbols in different canvas shapes in various positions. Landscape motifs are of course naturally adaptable to these structures but you will find the portrait, figure and still life motifs can be incorporated beautifully with the multiple *I* structured diagonally. You must guard against the triangle forms and funnels that will result from the diagonal placement. Compensate for these negative areas by using additional structure lines to hold the forms into the canvas surface.

ILLUSTRATION 52

MULTIPLE PARALLEL T

The *T* symbols are set in a parallel
pattern through a narrow vertical shape to form
an interesting positive pattern. You will note
that *L* and *O* shapes have been created
in the background.
This structural pattern is most adaptable to
exterior and interior building motifs
because of the strong parallel pattern. The
pattern can also be adapted to abstract still life
painting or traditional landscape.
You should experiment with the multiple
T idea by reversing light and shade
and by combining both light and dark *T*
symbols in the same pattern. Be aware of the
additional symbols that invariably
are created in the background areas. One
symbol should dominate the surface and all
others should be subjected to that letter.
Keep the pattern predominantly in right angle
positioning to the periphery lines
and inner thrust of the letters. Disperse the
light and dark areas equally over the surface to
insure adequate contrast in the structure.

ILLUSTRATION 53

MULTIPLE PARALLEL L

You are looking at another pattern extremely
adaptable to buildings, doorways and
window motifs. The structure is created by
the combining of two light *L* symbols with two
dark *L* structure symbols. The dominant
L symbol is in the light center area.
Other structure lines would be undoubtedly
added to support a building motif.
These must be held in the same attitude as the
basic structure idea. The light and dark
L symbols are almost equal in space
consumption with the light slightly dominant.
You can reverse this pattern with equal success.
Experiment with the light and dark
L symbols in many attitudes and
in different canvas sizes, both in horizontal
and vertical positions.
The *L*'s can also be set in diagonal
patterns. You will have some antagonizing shapes
resulting but they can be corrected if you
are aware of their presence. The
diagonal patterns will be more dramatic than
the formal arrangement you see here.
Remember, the *L* is a natural structural pattern
which can be recognized in the structure of
paintings all through the ages. The *L* structure
contains all the ingredients for constructing a
sound scaffolding for a composition.
Its extreme versatility makes it
applicable to contemporary expression.

ILLUSTRATION 54

MULTIPLE DIAGONAL AND PARALLEL X

For the first time the pattern is both
diagonal and parallel. This is a dangerous
structural idea unless you keep in mind
that the dominant expression must be either one
or the other—never both.
The light *X* is dominating the surface in this
complicated structure pattern. The
distorted dark *X* symbols are placed in a
parallel position in the upper portion of
the surface. Note that none of the symbols strike
into a corner. They are unified and
overlapping. The symbols lose their identity
as letters and act as an abstract idea.
Additional light and dark shapes could cut into
the existing pattern depending on the
development of the motif idea. Success with
a complicated structure idea depends
upon the careful knitting of the motif into
the structural pattern.
Abstract and nonobjective painters can utilize
such patterns with very little effort.
Color and textural accents can be overlaid
to control the eye movement on the surface
without additional rhythm symbols.

ILLUSTRATION 55

MULTIPLE PARALLEL O (□)

The *O*'s are placed in block form into a
horizontal rectangular shape. You can already
see a building motif suggested by the
shape relationships. Once understanding
has been reached as to the basic structure
purpose, you can experiment with the
motif and structure in a single process, keeping
in mind all the compositional principles.
A good foundation of knowledge and
experience must exist before you can expect
successful results. You must conscientiously
work to eliminate all structural problems before
the actual laying on of paint begins.
The advantages of a multiple *O* structure
pattern are tremendous. The *O*'s
can be utilized as surface light over other
structural symbols such as *Y*'s, *X*'s, or *L*'s. This
means that by situating a square
of light over an existing structure pattern you
are adding another dimension to the
design. To gain the most from the *O* symbol
you must consider it both as a single structure
idea and in combination with all other symbols.

ILLUSTRATION 56

COMBINING PARALLEL X AND I

For the first time you see two different letters
deliberately combined to form the structure
pattern. As you can perceive, the possibilities are
extensive. The important rule to remember is
to keep one letter dominant in the surface
and let all additional symbols be subjected to it.
The illustration denotes a light, off
center *X* stretched through the surface and
binding to the light *I*. The *X* is bound
to the second, third and fourth periphery lines.

It is a tightly knit structure that is successful
in any position and on any size or shape.
The emotional impact of the pattern is forceful
even though it is formally arranged.
It is adaptable to all styles of painting and
will accept a tremendous range of motif ideas.
Experiment with the *X* and *I* symbols
and multiples of them. Use both light and
dark symbols in the same structure
employing varying patterns and shapes.
Add some minor diagonal accents,
keeping in mind that the right angle parallel
structure is dominant.

ILLUSTRATION 57

COMBINATION DIAGONAL X
AND MULTIPLE PARALLEL I

The diagonal *X* and parallel *I*'s have been deliberately designed in the same surface to produce harmonious horizontal structure. The *X* is dominant in the pattern, consuming the majority of the allotted space. Although it is not touching the second or fourth periphery lines, it could be designed to do so. In the top dark pattern the *X* is placed off center and appears in the middle of the lower illustration. This pattern, in a horizontal position, is an automatic landscape structure. An *S* symbol can be superimposed to lend movement and perspective. Turned to a vertical position, the design produces an extremely dramatic effect. It is more suited now for figure and still life motifs. Do not overlook the adaptation to abstract motif ideas. It can also be incorporated successfully into an interior or street scene motif.

ILLUSTRATION 58

COMBINING DIAGONAL Y
AND PARALLEL I

Here is another structure pattern utilizing two
opposing forces. The diagonal *Y* dominates
the surface with a strong though less powerful *I*
symbol binding the number four periphery
line. The background shapes created
need some assistance to hold them into
the surface and prevent the eye from funneling
out of the canvas.
The emotional impact in the vertical position
is great and lessens when it is used in
the horizontal position. Seen vertically, it is
extremely adaptable to a floral idea but
becomes a landscape in the horizontal position.
Experiment with this structural idea
allowing parallel *I*'s to dominate and the *Y*
to fall into a position of lesser importance.
Never equalize the diagonal and parallel forces or
you will establish a competitive relationship.
Change the canvas shape and employ
both light and dark symbols in the same design.

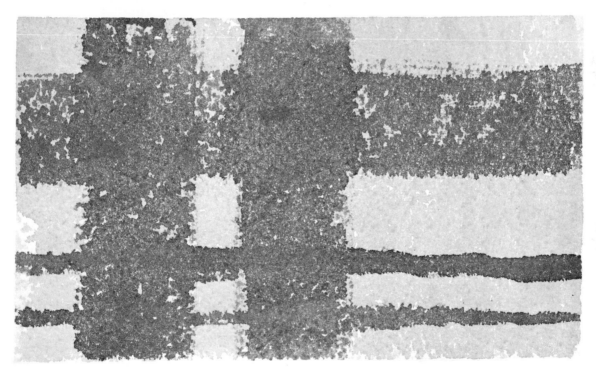

ILLUSTRATION 59

*COMBINING DIAGONAL
AND PARALLEL H'S AND I'S*

This two part illustration enables you to see
both diagonal and parallel structures built with
the *H* and *I* symbols in combination.
In the top illustration you are seeing a
diagonal placement of the letters but the patterns
are running parallel to each other. Experiment
with this idea by setting the lines at
variance. The total emotional concept will change.

The bottom pattern utilizes the *H* and *I*
symbols in a parallel placement both
to each other and to the periphery lines. It is a
formal organized structure of tremendous
versatility. It is suitable for adaptation
to building and street scene motifs, landscapes
and still lifes, figures and heads, all
with equal success.
Many variations of this structure idea can
be composed by reversing light and
shade, changing the placement of the symbols
and by designing the patterns on various
shapes in both horizontal and vertical positions.

89

ILLUSTRATION 60

COMBINING PARALLEL T AND I

The dark *T* is dominant in this structural design
and is stretched through the total surface,
touching all four of the periphery lines. The
I is acting as a structural support in
back of the large upside down *T*. The pattern
is constructed with right angles and
parallels expressing a dramatic emotion
simply because of the vertical positioning of the
shape. When it is placed in a horizontal
position, the attitude is formal and restful.
This structural idea can be further
extended by changing the shape of the
canvas and converting the light and shade
pattern. Experiment with these two
symbols by reversing the dominating letters and
rearrange the positions of the symbols.
The structure is an automatic
foundation for a floral or figure motif. It can
also relate to a building idea such
as a doorway. Throw a light *O* onto the
center area and emphasize abstract
light placement over the structure. Such
manipulation will extend the
value of the *T* and *I* in combination.

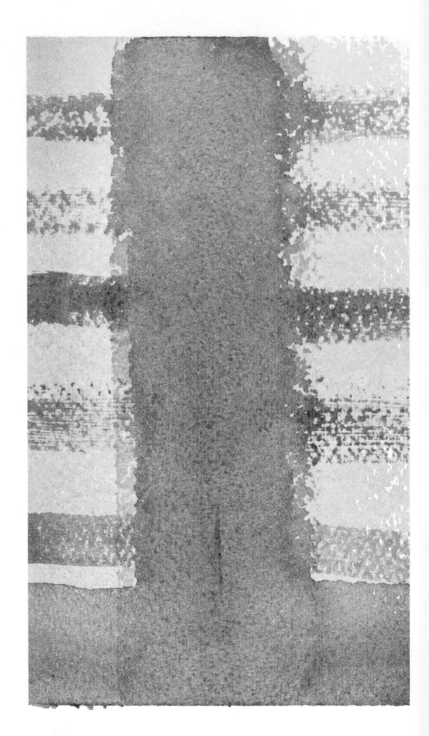

ILLUSTRATION 61

COMBINING PARALLEL T
AND DIAGONAL Y

In this illustration the parallel *T* acts as support
for the dominant *Y* symbol. The
pattern is intriguing and works well except
for the small light triangular shape at
the top. This can be corrected by adding
a parallel or diagonal accent that
bisects the shape. The pattern
suggests a table and wall surface created
by the *T* and a bouquet shape by the *Y*, making

it more suitable for still life or abstract
motifs than landscape or figure ideas.
Experiment with multiples of the two
symbols, keeping in mind that either
the *T* or *Y* must dominate the surface. When
two or more letters are used the symbols
lose their identity and act as
an abstract design. The more complicated
the structure becomes the more difficult it is
to relate the motif effectively. Once you
have established a good structure
idea, do not allow disintegration of it
during the application of the subject idea.

ILLUSTRATION 62

COMBINING PARALLEL L'S AND O

This dual illustration shows the positioning
of light and dark *L*'s and a rectangular *O*. It is
an extremely simple structural idea
and will support any type of motif idea.
A figure can be superimposed over the
structure and held tightly. Edgar Degas often
structured his figure paintings with
this tool. The structure seems to be equally
adaptable to street scenes and building
motifs. Again, a still life motif composed with
many objects can be set over the surface and
the strong binding quality of the
structure will hold them in position.
Experiment with the *L* and *O* symbols by
reversing light and shade, combining
both light and dark symbols, and by changing
the canvas shape and position. You can
also set the symbols in a diagonal pattern
if you compensate for the triangular
shapes that will be created.

ILLUSTRATION 63

COMBINING PARALLEL X, L *AND* I'S

This structural pattern was established
by placing *X, L* and *I*'s in a parallel design. You
are looking at three different symbols
in combination for the first time. The symbols
have lost their identity as such and operate
now as a solid abstract shape. All space is positive
and held to the periphery lines. The
structure is adaptable especially to still life
motifs and abstract painting. A design,
incorporating more than two symbols, has a
tendency to become complicated, making
the adaptation of a theme very difficult. Be
careful to maintain the structure.
Do not allow the motif to alter the light
and dark dispersion or the main thrust
of the structure.
Experiment with these three symbols in both
parallel and diagonal patterns by
reversing the light and dark areas and
placing them in different shapes and positions.

ILLUSTRATION 64

COMBINING PARALLEL T AND I'S WITH DIAGONAL X

The structure pattern now is formed with two
parallel symbols and a small diagonal *X*.
The dark *T* is the dominant force supported by
strong dark and light *I* symbols. The
structure is adaptable to still life, nonobjective
and abstract motifs. Experimental work
with these three letters in combination will
produce complicated and varied structural ideas.
Set the *X* and *I*'s in diagonal positioning
and the *T* in a parallel, reverse light and shade
in the symbols and change the canvas
shape and position. Experiment with any
multiples of three letters in both
diagonal and vertical positions to understand the
endless source of structural ideas.

ILLUSTRATION 65

OVERLAY OF DIAGONAL X, L, *AND* H

Your exercises should now be directed
towards combining the symbols by
laying one over another. The letters lose their
identity and you create pleasing abstract patterns.
This example illustrates the diagonal *X*
dominating and stretching over ¾ of
the canvas surface. The *L* and *H* are partially
placed over the large dark *X* creating an
intriguing design. Experiment with
several different and like symbols in
overlay, keeping in mind the four rules
of sound structure:

1. One letter should dominate all others
2. Light and dark dispersion should
   almost equalize
3. Parallel or diagonal emphasis should dominate
   —never both!
4. All resulting shapes must be positive

ILLUSTRATION 66

OVERLAY OF PARALLEL H, O *AND* L

This illustration shows three letters in overlay,
all paralleling each other and the
periphery lines. Experiment with the
straight line symbols in multiples of three.
Interlace them by overlaying them
on top of each other, maintaining one dominant
symbol. Reverse the light and dark patterns,
change shapes and sizes and keep in
mind the structural rules.

You should now be incorporating rough
motif ideas in relationship to the structure.
Remember, the motif is developed
after the designing of the structure. The motif
can suggest a suitable pattern but
must never be allowed to usurp the structural
design. Do not allow disintegration of the
structure during the process of applying the motif.
All symbols, whether they be used
in singles or multiples, parallel or diagonally,
in horizontal or vertical shapes are
applicable tools. You must select the relationships
which best suit your personal needs.

ILLUSTRATION 67

SINGLE S

This two part illustration denotes the placement
of the *S* symbol in horizontal and
vertical shapes. The structure has been
eliminated and only the surface
rhythm appears on the canvas shapes.
The *X* represents the focal point areas. Note
that the focal point is incorporated into the
rhythmical letter. When in actual application the
focal point area will carry the strongest
color accent of the composition. The same
color will be repeated at least three
times over the *S* rhythm to sustain and
control the eye movement.
The *S* is held within the surface and
need not touch the periphery edge.
It is superimposed over the already developed
structure pattern but is not necessarily an
ingredient in every structure. Some patterns
sustain the surface rhythm without it;
however, it is a great designing aid when
it is properly applied.
This exercise was planned to increase
the awareness of surface rhythm and focal point
placement. Experiment with the single *S*
in various sizes and shapes and in different
positions within the canvas shape.

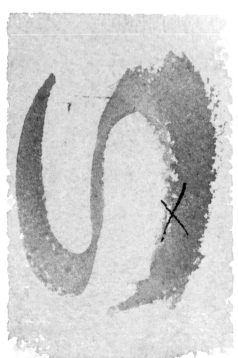

ILLUSTRATION 68

MULTIPLE C

Here you see that the half circle or the *C* symbol
housed in a square and a rectangular
space. Again the structure has been removed and
only the rhythm and the focal point area
appear on the surface. A *single C* is not an
adequate rhythm symbol because the
thrust of a single *C* has no counter rhythm
to control eye movement. The *C* should
be considered only in multiples. When three or
more are used the symbol can then be placed
over the surface to insure rhythm

control of the space. The *C* symbols need
not touch the periphery unless it is desired.
The curved symbols are not intended
to be stamped on the surface in a completed work.
They represent basic rhythm planning and
are to be distorted so they are almost invariably
lost in the final development of a
composition. In actual application the focal
point will contain the strongest value
in the color composition and must be repeated at
least three times on the symbol line.
Experiment with the halfmoon shape by
changing its position on the surface
and by utilizing various canvas shapes. Establish
a focal point in all of your exercises.

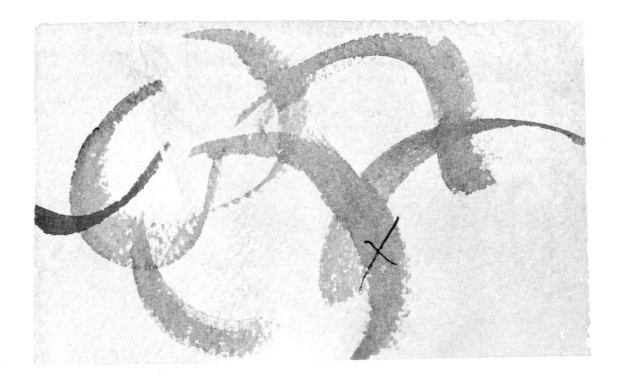

ILLUSTRATION 69

COMBINING S *AND* C

This dual illustration denotes the *S* and *C*
symbols incorporated in the same rhythm pattern.
The symbols lose their identity as such
and move together in a rhythmical pattern.
The focal point is located within the
massive *S* movement but it need not be as
long as it is incorporated into a strong rhythm line.
Experiment with the *S* and *C* symbols
by changing positions of the symbols and
placing them into various sizes and
shapes. Remember, that the symbols are intended
only to develop a firm sense of rhythm in a
structure form and need not appear on
the surface of the completed work. You
are teaching yourself to establish deliberate eye
movement over the painting surface. This
can be done with a single *S* symbol
or multiples of *C* and again by combining
the two rhythms within a single structure pattern.

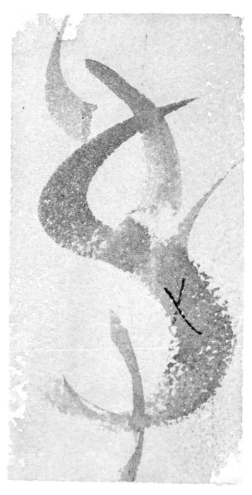

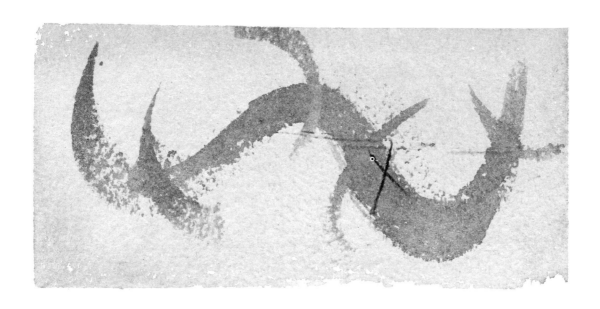

ILLUSTRATION 70

SINGLE S *WITH MOTIF*

The *S* is employed here not only as a surface
rhythm pattern but as a deliberate designing aid.
The blooms of the flowers are concentrated
on the rhythm line thus assuring a
pleasing arrangement of the blooms. The
straight lines of the stems fall naturally
into a varied and intriguing pattern. The *X*
represents the focal point area, in this
case, an actual bloom. Such conscious placement
of objects in a composition prevents many
an inadvertent error of arrangement. Both the
S and the *C* symbols can be employed
in this manner. Do not confuse this designing
principle with structure! It is only directed
to object arrangement and does not
relate to light and dark dispersion.
The same principle of object arrangement is
applicable to all motif ideas. Experiment
with the *S* and *C* symbols in direct relationship
with objects. Use different rhythm
patterns in various shapes and sizes and
with extensive motif ideas.

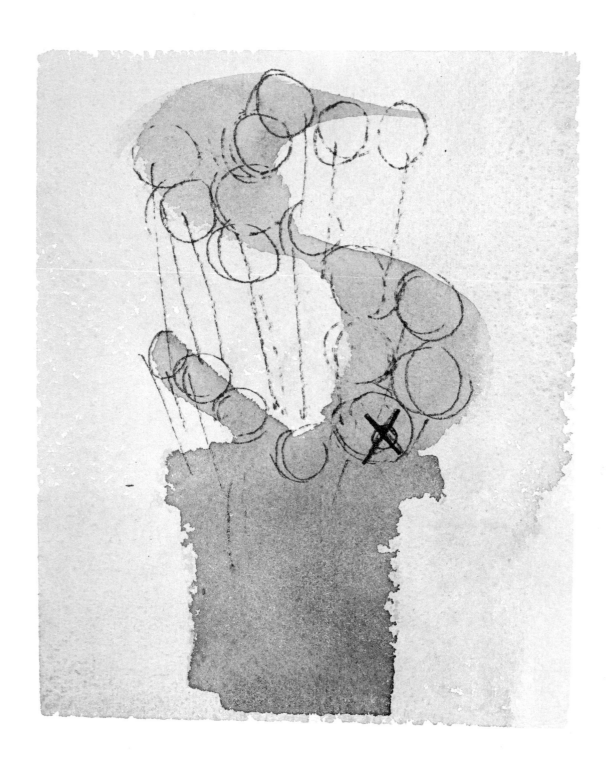

ILLUSTRATION 71-A

SINGLE PARALLEL DARK X WITH PORTRAIT CARTOON OVERLAY

Your experiments with the letter symbols should
now be well established in your thought
processes. It is time to adapt the theme, the
subject idea, to your structure pattern.
Here you see a single dark X stretched in
a parallel pattern through the total surface.
A drawing of a head has been placed
over the structure. This was
done so that you can identify the
light and dark dispersion with clarity.
You should do the same. Use tissue or transfer
paper. Draw a rough cartoon of a subject
idea and lay it over several structural ideas.
Choose the most compatible structures
and adapt the motif to them. You can introduce
light and dark shapes when the motif demands
it. Do not allow the addition of light
and dark accents to destroy the abstract
structure pattern that is under the
motif. Light shapes can be introduced into
the X pattern but the massive X must
be maintained in order to prevent deterioration
of the structure force.
The head is situated so that the hair touches
the number one, two and four periphery
lines with the neck conforming to the X on
the number three line. Triangles have
been formed in the upper left and right corners.
These shapes must be adjusted (either now
or in the final painting) by dropping
the line of the hair or by maintaining the
exact light pattern of the background.

ILLUSTRATION 71-B

PEGGY—5″ x 6½″

This small painting of PEGGY was executed
in the oil technique introduced in Section
VIII. The dark X structure lies underneath the
painting and can be identified by the
umber glazes running through the head and
resting on the four periphery lines.
Light was directed from the left, placing
the front facial planes in light. The light pattern
is not great enough to disintegrate
the X structure that houses the head.
The background is gold leaf and ·
has been antiqued with umber glazes. The
effect is that of a light background surrounding
the head motif. Dark glazes were intensified
in the upper left and right corners to
hold the light pattern as square shapes rather
than triangles.

ILLUSTRATION 72-A

*SINGLE PARALLEL DARK X WITH
STREET SCENE CARTOON OVERLAY*

Again we are looking at a dark *X* stretched
in a parallel pattern through the total painting
surface. The motif is changed from a head
to a street scene. The *X* serves both subjects with
equal power. The difference is that the
light areas are dominating the surface in
the street scene while in the portrait illustration
the darks are supreme. The single *X*
used in this manner is the simplest type
of structure ideas.
The shadow pattern of the building is actually
identifiable as the structural *X* symbol.
It is not disturbed by any
introduction of lights in the massive shape.
All space, both in the subject and the
background is positive and balanced. The
shapes are presenting interesting relationships.
The stairway acts as a horizontal
contrast to the vertical building structure.
The focal point is located in the right
center front and represented by the weeds
and steps.

ILLUSTRATION 72-B

STAIRWAY—16″ x 20″

The painting STAIRWAY was designed
from the simple dark parallel *X* structure. The
dark pattern represents buildings in
shadow and cast shadows on the stairway and
can be easily identified in the final work.
Burnt sienna, umber, and ultramarine
blue glazes were painted over an acrylic
underpainting in all of the dark areas. The light
pattern carries white, pink and ochre
oil passages. The underpainting is visible in
a large area in the light shapes and
under the transparent dark oil glazes in
the structure pattern.
The strongest color in the painting is the hot
reddish-brown burnt sienna glaze. This
appears in the weeds and steps in the focal
point area and is repeated in a rhythmic pattern
in the roof and doorways of the buildings.

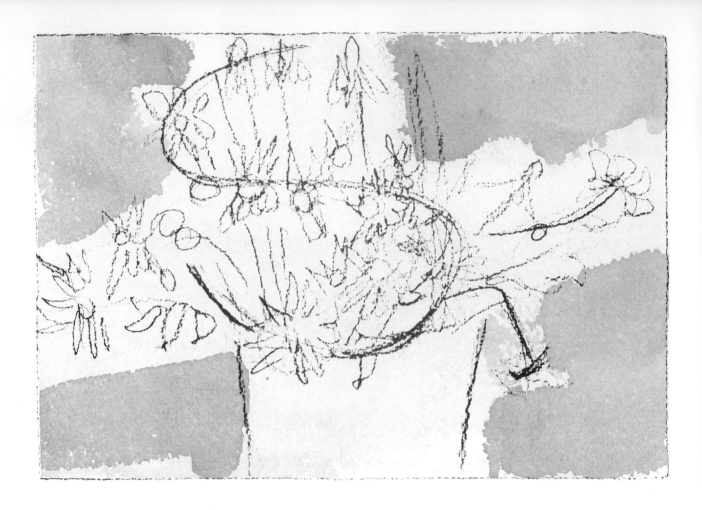

ILLUSTRATION 73-A

SINGLE DIAGONAL LIGHT X
WITH S *RHYTHM SYMBOL*
AND FLORAL CARTOON OVERLAY

Here is a light diagonal X pattern that has
been stretched through the total painting surface.
The floral sketch has been
laid over the light structure pattern.
The S rhythm symbol was incorporated
to lend order to the designing of the blooms
and stems of the motif. The focal point
has been placed at the left, center front and on
the S rhythm line.
Again the subject conforms completely
with the light X structure pattern. The
background areas are held in positive shape
because of the light interruption of
the loosely designed X. No triangular shapes were
created in the four corners of the surface.
All possible negative areas have been rehabilitated
and the total composition is successful.

ILLUSTRATION 73-B

FLOWERS—*18″ X 24″*

FLOWERS was executed on board using the
technique described in Section VIII.
The color scheme is white, yellow and orange
contrasted with a recessive turquoise color
in the background. Hansa yellow light is
the strongest color in the painting and appears in
its brightest passage in the focal point area
which, in this case, is a large yellow daisy. The
yellow is moved in an S rhythm through
the center areas of the painting. Orange, white
and accents of blue were used in the floral
motif creating a warm, forward movement in the
flowers. An opaque turquoise color made
from combining thalo blue and green with
white was painted into a wet ultramarine
glaze. The background is strong, bright
and dark and holds the warm, light bouquet
securely in position.

ILLUSTRATION 74-A

THREE DIAGONAL DARK Y'S WITH TREE CARTOON OVERLAY

Three *Y*'s were designed in a diagonal overlapping pattern to suggest a rather abstract tree idea. Tissue paper was then laid over the structure pattern and the sketch drawn to conform to the dark pattern underneath. Some additional diagonal shapes were added to increase the effectiveness of the subject idea but not enough to disturb the original structure concept. The focal point is located in the lower left, center front and is emphasized by the introduction of lines intended to carry textural pattern. The small negative shapes created in the background areas must be rehabilitated with a change of color values in the final work.

ILLUSTRATION 74-B

TREE—*28″ X 46″*

This large oil painting was executed on canvas using an underpainting technique. The rich, warm reddish-browns of the tree are contrasting with a light, bright recessive blue sky. Again, the tree shape is conforming almost identically with the structural pattern of the three diagonal dark *Y*'s. The focal point area is identified by textural emphasis suggesting tree bark in the lower left, center front. Textural patterns were carried into the heavy branches of the tree to aid in the eye movement over the surface.

Burnt sienna and umber glazes were painted over a light orange and yellow underpainting of the *Y* forms. The background was underpainted in shades of green and blue. Thalo blue and white were combined to create a strong blue sky color and painted into a wet blue glaze. Several hues of the blue opaque sky color were used to hold the negative background shapes into the picture plane. They are still negative in shape but are so treated by the tonal color change that they are bound to the periphery lines. Such color treatment holds the eye into the painting and allows the viewer to enjoy the total work.

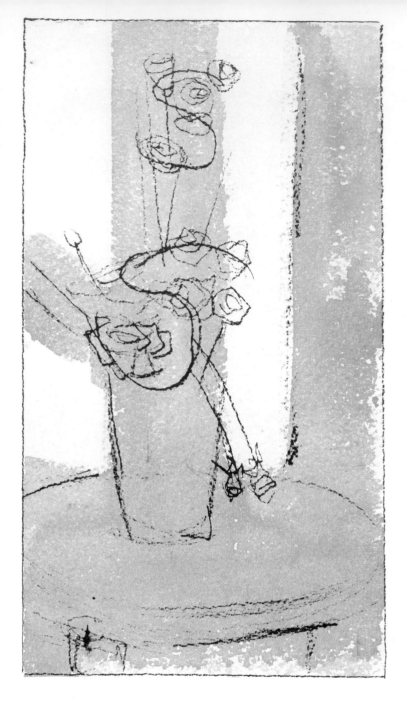

ILLUSTRATION 75-A

DARK PARALLEL L, DARK DIAGONAL Y AND S RHYTHM SYMBOLS WITH A FLORAL CARTOON OVERLAY

In this illustration you are seeing a dark *L* binding the number three and four periphery lines. A large light *O* is formed in the remaining space. Over this space, a dark diagonal *Y* was placed. The diagonal emphasis is subjected to the dominant parallel structure. An overlay sketch describes the floral motif which includes a circular table. Two *S* symbols were used to design the blooms and stem arrangement. The focal point is located in the lower left front area and rests on the larger *S* symbol. All areas are positive. The structure consumes the total space; the light and dark dispersion is close to equalization and the motif has been successfully coordinated with the underlying structure.

ILLUSTRATION 75-B

ROSES—16″ X 36″

ROSES was painted on a canvas surface using an underpainting. Red is the dominant color and it is located in its strongest value at the focal point which is seen as a large red rose in the lower left, center front. The color is moved through the surface as blooms. Red and orange also appear in the warm table area in small color passages. The wall in back of the flowers has been painted grey-blue on the dark side. The table is part of the dark *L* but moves forward in the finished work because of the warm burnt sienna glazes that were laid over a pink and orange underpainting. Sap green was the glaze over a yellow leaf underpainting while alizarine crimson and cadmium orange glazes were painted in transparent passages over the flowers. The dark linear emphasis in the design was executed with ultramarine blue and sap green to correlate the blue-grey wall with the floral motif.

ILLUSTRATION 76-A

SINGLE PARALLEL DARK T WITH FIGURE CARTOON OVERLAY

This structure was designed to house a
portrait of my young son, Brice. A dark T shape
was stretched through the surface, touching
all four periphery edges. The cartoon
was sketched on transparent paper and laid over
the simple one letter structure.
Since the painting was planned in tonal
values of blues and executed primarily
in a drawing technique, the figure was cut
below the knee. This is permissible only when the
painting is designed as a one color statement.
The focal point is located slightly left
of center front and is represented by the
shirt area. The rhythm is carried
only by the drawing as it moves up and
down vertically in the design.

ILLUSTRATION 76-B

BRICE—24″ X 36″

The portrait of BRICE was executed on canvas
utilizing a blue acrylic toned ground. The
technique is explained completely in Section VIII.
The figure was overlaid on an imaginary
upside down T. Light direction is from
the left and invades the dark T structure. This
invasion cuts the dark percentage and
allows the light to dominate the surface. The
T structure is identified by the figure itself
that touches the number one and three periphery
lines. The grass carries a
pale ochre glaze over the blue toned ground
and stretches the width of the canvas.
A three dimensional effect has been created
by the almost white opaques of the light
side contrasting with the more recessive blue
glazes on the dark side of the figure. The
sky was painted by covering that area
with a thin glaze of ultramarine and umber.
The cloud areas were lifted out with cheesecloth,
exposing the toned ground underneath.
The entire work is held with the loose fluid sepia
chalk drawing that was placed directly
onto the toned surface. A few additional line
accents were drawn with burnt sienna
to enhance the portrait in the final stage.

113

ILLUSTRATION 77-A

PARALLEL DARK T
AND DARK AND LIGHT I*'S*
WITH PORTRAIT CARTOON OVERLAY

This structure design is extremely complicated
in its concept. The dark upside down parallel *T*
is stretched through the surface touching
the number one and three periphery lines.
The *T* is intended to house a head and
shoulder motif. The striped background is formed
by utilizing light and dark *I*'s. The massive
light *I* on the left is conforming with the
lighting of the head and shoulders while the
large dark *I* supports the dark side of the figure.
The side planes of the head
and front planes of the shoulder appear in
light, invading the dark *T* and causing
the *T* to lose its identity as a symbol. The dark,
however, binds the head and shoulders so
that disintegration of structure does not occur.

ILLUSTRATION 77-B

MARY—*12″ X 16″*

The painting of MARY was executed on canvas,
utilizing a blue toned ground. The cartoon
for the head and figure was then drawn directly
on the canvas with chalk and fixed with hair spray.
Recessive blue and green
glazes were next painted over the background
area and the figure glazed with warm umber and
sienna glazes which moved the figure
forward in the picture plane. Because of
the blue underlying toned ground, the total
surface has a subdued tonal quietude
in keeping with the attitude of the figure.
A few opaque passages appear on the surface in
the large light *I* on the left and in
the light side of the figure. The blue color
of the ground is in evidence through the
total surface, lending a unity
and spontaneity to the painting.

ILLUSTRATION 78-A

DIAGONAL H *AND PARALLEL* I'S
WITH SHELL CARTOON OVERLAY

The *H* symbol has been placed at an angle
in the surface and is touching the number two,
three and four periphery lines. The
sea shells and driftwood were sketched into the
dark *H* structure form with the *S* symbol
conforming to the same pattern. The *I*'s
were placed in a horizontal
position and represent sky and sea area.
There are no negative areas in this composition
despite the diagonal *H* pattern. The parallel
I's are held so abstractly that they
do not overpower the diagonal force of
the *H* symbol. It is evident that the
identical structure could be attained by
employing the diagonal *X* and *I* in combination.

ILLUSTRATION 78-B

SEA AND SHELLS—*16″ X 20″*

SEA AND SHELLS was executed on canvas
employing an acrylic underpainting. The
color scheme is dominantly cool, using blue, green
and white in the sky, sea and sand
areas. The *H* structure carries the shell
motif and is dominated by ochre,
orange and pink. The pink color is in the focal
point area and is carried by the *S* symbol
through the remaining shells and driftwood.
Textural emphasis has been added to the shells
and driftwood in the same *S* rhythm.
All the objects are united by blue and green
glazes, lending a cool wet look to the
surface. The light *I* at the number
one periphery line is static and relieves
the action of the surf and the
abstract rhythm of the shells and driftwood.

ILLUSTRATION 79-A

*PARALLEL DARK AND LIGHT I'S
WITH A FIGURE CARTOON OVERLAY*

The dark and light *I*'s are stretched through
a narrow vertical surface and a cartoon of a nude
was placed over the structure pattern.
The massive light *I* in the center of the surface
accommodates the vertically positioned figure.
The long hair conforms to the dark *I* of
the left side of the figure while the *I*'s to the right
support the shadow side of the figure.
The focal point is now radically changed
and appears in the head area. The light
side of the hair and side facial planes will identify
the entrance and exit of the eye.
The rhythm moves up and down in a
vertical attitude through the figure.

ILLUSTRATION 79-B

YOUTH—*12″ X 24″*

YOUTH was painted on a canvas utilizing
a blue and ochre underpainting. The hair was
underpainted in tones of ochre and white
while the head, figure and background were
underpainted with shades of light blue.
The color scheme in the final oil painting is green
due to the sap green glazes that were
painted over the total surface. A blue tint
from the underpainting can be seen
through the burnt sienna and sap green
glazes on the flesh. Burnt sienna was also painted
in thin passages over the hair area. The
warm glazes pull the figure forward while the
green moves back on the canvas plane.
The focal point is controlled by the light
area of the head and hair and
begins the vertical rhythm through the canvas.

ILLUSTRATION 80-A

DARK AND LIGHT PARALLEL I'S
AND S RHYTHM
WITH FIGURE CARTOON OVERLAY

The vertical shape is again structured with
dark and light paralleling *I*'s but the arrangement
of the *I*'s creates a different pattern
to that of illustration 79-A. The figure is
now superimposed over the dark massive *I*
in the center of the surface. The lights
of the figure are intruding upon
this dark shape but not enough to destroy
its strong structural force.
The focal point is located at the elbow
of the child and is carried by the *S* rhythm
symbol through the painting. The dark *I*
on the right supports the shadow side of the
figure while the light *I* on the
left allows for the lighting of the figure.

ILLUSTRATION 80-B

DEBORAH—*16" X 30"*

DEBORAH was painted on canvas, utilizing a
pale pink ground color. The same color
is in evidence through the total work. The
cartoon was drawn directly onto the
canvas surface from the model in sepia chalk. The
drawing was fixed with hair spray and the burnt
sienna glazes painted over the total
surface. The painting is extremely warm
because of the pink toned ground and
the hot glazing color. A blue glaze made from
mixing burnt sienna and ultramarine blue
appears in the dark *I* on the right of the
canvas. This aids in the three dimensional effect.
Pink, ochre and white scumbles
were painted in the light side of the figure.
The focal point at the elbow carries tones
of light pink which is the brightest color in the
painting and is repeated throughout
the costume and face of the child.
The figure assumes a natural relaxed attitude
and is dressed in a simple classic costume.
The hair was designed in a classic ponytail style
and held well away from the head oval
and neck cylinder.

121

ILLUSTRATION 81-A

*DARK AND LIGHT PARALLEL I'S
AND S SYMBOL
WITH FIGURE CARTOON OVERLAY*

Again the illustration is a parallel *I* structure
that has been stretched through the total
canvas in a vertical position. The cartoon overlay
is that of a distorted nude figure. The
focal point is located in the abdomen and is
resting on the *S* symbol. The *I*'s to the
right support the vertically placed figure
and symbolize a striped drape in the background
of the painting. The light *I* to the
left supports the figure and lends a static
area to the work.

ILLUSTRATION 81-B

WHITE NUDE—*12″ X 16″*

This small painting is highly stylized and
decorative. It was executed on an underpainting
of white, green and pink acrylic paint.
The figure carries light green oil glazes and
white opaques scumbled into the figure mass.
Burnt sienna glazes were painted over
the hair and into the light stripes on the right in
the background area. A glaze of ultramarine
blue was painted over the costume and
dark stripes of the background. The dark *I*
to the right was conditioned with a
green opaque pulling the mass to a middle tone
color. The painting is cool in its total
effect. The minor pink accents add a highly
decorative quality to the work.

ILLUSTRATION 82-A

PARALLEL DARK AND LIGHT I'S
WITH FIGURE CARTOON OVERLAY

In this illustration the light *I* controls the
majority of the canvas space. The two *I*'s, one
light and one dark of different widths,
have been stretched vertically through a narrow
surface. The *I* symbols could be read as light
and dark *O*'s or light and dark rectangles as well.
The figure motif has been simply placed
in the center of the surface.
The light and dark dispersion of the
underlying structure can be clearly identified
under the sketch overlay. The intent is
to hold the light and dark dispersion in
the final painting much as it appears in this
structure and cartoon illustration. Such
treatment is perhaps the simplest
of compositional ideas and can be applied with
equal success to portrait painting.

ILLUSTRATION 82-B

SEATED CHILD—*16″ X 28″*

The painting was executed on a pale blue-green
acrylic toned ground. An impression
of the model was drawn directly on the canvas
surface with chalk. The cartoon was fixed
and oil glazes painted in thin passages
over the total surface. The light side of the figure
was partially relieved of the dark glazes
and pale ochre and white scumbles were
applied to increase the three dimensional
effect. The chair was held in an understatement
and serves as a necessary prop.
The dark glazes in the right structural *I* were
deepened to support the figure and bind it
into place. The total color effect is blue
with minor ochre scumbles in the light areas of
the head and costume. The linear accents
were added to enhance the fluid, sketchy
appearance of the painting.

ILLUSTRATION 83-A

PARALLEL LIGHT AND DARK I'S WITH FIGURE OVERLAY

This structure pattern is identical to the previous
example (82-A) except that the size of
the support is changed and the intent of the
painting procedure differs greatly. The
cartoon of the figure is placed completely in the
light area and only just touches the dark
I line. Such positioning of the figure implies
that the dark shadow side of the figure
will be held in a lighter key than
the dark *I* on the right of the surface.
By maintaining this plan, the light and
dark dispersion of the structure can be held
intact. Variations of this structure
can be seen in abundance in the work
of figure and portrait painters of the past.

ILLUSTRATION 83-B

PAPER DOLLS—22″ X 28″

The simple *I* structure supports a highly
colored painting. The light and shade of the head,
arms and hands were underpainted in
two tones of ochre, umber and white. The
dress was toned with a pink. The paper
dolls were underpainted in a bluish grey;
the light side of the background was
painted in a pale yellow and the dark side with
a dull green. A light blue halo was painted
in an erratic pattern about the head
and figure and along the edge of the green
background mass.
Burnt sienna oil glazes were painted over the hair,
flesh and dress areas. The glazes were
lifted off on the light side of the figure and
opaque lights were added. White and
blue opaques were scumbled into the paper dolls.
The paper dolls were held in an understatement
so that they would not overpower the figure
of the child. A yellow glaze was followed
by a lighter yellow opaque in the area behind
the figure. An ultramarine glaze
covered the dark green background area;
into the wet glaze was scumbled a dark
green, leaving some of the blue glaze exposed
on the surface.
The cool blue color in the background
and about the figure was used to relieve and
complement the intense red color of
the figure and strong yellow background.
The colors would have been too
intense and unrelated except for the unification
created by the blue color accents.

ILLUSTRATION 84-A

*PARALLEL LIGHT AND DARK O'S
WITH LANDSCAPE
AND FIGURE CARTOON OVERLAY*

A simple structure pattern
was adopted for this illustration. The parallel
light and dark O's have been placed in
a horizontal position and a landscape cartoon
overlaid. The dark *O* becomes the sky and
the light *O* assumes the ground area.
The figure is subjugated completely
to the landscape motif and its addition does
not enter into the structure pattern at all.
Its only purpose is to enhance the motif idea and
give a rule of measure to the landscape.
A building, animals or trees could be adapted
with ease to such a structure idea. The light
and dark shapes can be reversed with
equal success and additional structure and rhythm
symbols added to support
a multitude of landscape motifs.

ILLUSTRATION 84-B

CHILD IN A FIELD—*30" X 40"*

This large simple canvas was executed utilizing
an underpainting technique. The sky was
underpainted in a pale blue, while the child
and field were done in shades of yellow
and white. The flowers in the field were drawn
in sepia chalk as was the contour of the child.
An ultramarine blue and burnt umber
oil glaze was painted over the sky area. The
cloud effect was achieved simply by
lifting off the glazes in a
cloud pattern. The figure carries
very few opaques and is held in an
understatement. The color from
the underpainting can be seen to a large
degree on the surface of the painting.

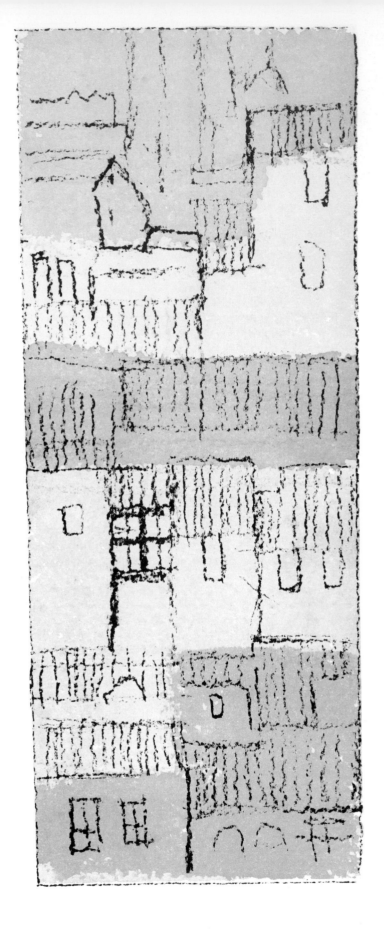

ILLUSTRATION 85-A

PARALLEL LIGHT AND DARK L'S AND DARK I WITH BUILDING CARTOON OVERLAY

The *L*'s and *I* are stretched horizontally through
a vertical surface. The structure pattern
is extremely acceptable to the building cartoon
suggested for adaptation.
The focal point is located in the lower right center
front and is carried strictly by the light pattern of
the structure. The light and dark dispersion
appears to be almost equal and
completely balanced. All space is positive
and bound securely to the periphery.
The light and dark pattern could be reversed
with ease or the structure rearranged to
create many additional composition patterns.

ILLUSTRATION 85-B

VIEW OF TAXCO—*16″ X 36″*

This rather abstract concept of the rooftops
of Taxco was executed on a canvas utilizing an
underpainting technique. All the light
areas were underpainted in white and ochre.
The rooftops were painted in tones of yellow. The
dark *L* structure was followed
and underpainted in blues and browns.
A drawing in chalk indicating windows, tile,
rooftops and the steepled
church was drawn over the underpainting
and fixed with hair spray.
Burnt sienna, Hansa yellow and cadmium
orange were painted in transparent passages over
the rooftops that conformed to the light
structure pattern. Ultramarine and burnt
umber were glazed over the dark
building and sky area, conforming completely
to the dark pattern of the structure.
Dark and light opaques were scumbled
into the corresponding areas where
structural emphasis was necessary. The
underpainting can be identified
to a great extent over the total surface.

ILLUSTRATION 86-A

PARALLEL DARK L AND LIGHT O
WITH FIGURE CARTOON OVERLAY

The versatile *L* is seen in this illustration
running in a vertical position and binding itself
to all four periphery lines. The dark *L*
is dominating the light *O* formed
in the upper left section of the canvas.
A complicated cartoon of a figure group
has been overlaid. The intent of the plan is to
hold the structure intact by adding lights only
where the motif demands three
dimensional identification.
The *L* and *O* present one of the simplest
of structure ideas and can be adapted to any
motif idea with assurance of success.

ILLUSTRATION 86-B

FAMILY—22″ X 36″

The cartoon for **FAMILY** was carefully
developed and transferred to a multicolor-toned
canvas. The figures were so arranged as to
insure the continuous rhythm of the painting.
The toned canvas carried abstract white,
blue, green and yellow colored shapes
and although the dark *L* dominates the surface,
these colors were kept in such pale tones
that the total work appears to be light.
The glazes were painted over the surface to
conform to the color in the underpainting
so that the abstract color pattern could
be maintained in the completed work.
The light *O* carries many pale opaque passages
that conform to the color of the underpainting.
The structure of this painting is
de-emphasized to project the motif. Still,
the structure is there and the figures are
held securely into the allotted space.

133

ILLUSTRATION 87-A

PARALLEL DARK H, *LIGHT AND DARK* I'S, S *AND* C *SYMBOLS WITH FLORAL AND FIGURE CARTOON OVERLAY*

This illustration depicts a complicated structure combined with an equally complicated motif. The *H* is placed in a horizontal position stretching through the width of the surface and contacting all four periphery lines. The *I*'s are subjected completely to the massive *H* and run in both vertical and horizontal positions. The light and dark dispersion appears to be almost equalized and all areas are positive. The cartoon overlay shows the figures and flower motif designed on the *H* structure lines. The focal point appears in the lower left section of the canvas on an *S* rhythm symbol. Additional *C* symbols are added to aid in the designing of the blooms and to insure the eye movement through the surface.

ILLUSTRATION 87-B

FLOWER SHOP— *30″ X 50″*

FLOWER SHOP was painted on canvas utilizing an underpainting technique. The yellow of the flowers at the focal point area is the strongest color on the painting surface and appears in a rhythmic pattern through the entire painting. The figures are held in positions by the dark blue-green background. The light paint of the figures invades the dark structure to some extent but not enough to disturb the structure. Warm glazes were painted over the figures and blooms of the flowers, moving them all forward in the surface. Recessive blue and green glazes were painted in the leaf and background areas and the blue-green color dominates the surface. Light scumbles were painted into the window and into the supporting *I*'s of the background to further promote the structure of the painting. Corresponding opaques were placed into the light side of the figures and into the flowers and containers. The figures are held in an understatement, allowing the floral motif to dominate the subject idea.

135

ILLUSTRATION 88-A

PARALLEL LIGHT AND DARK O'S,
DIAGONAL DARK Y'S,
LIGHT SURFACE O
WITH BUILDING CARTOON OVERLAY

The light and dark O's are the foundation
of the structure pattern and are set in a parallel
position. The two Y symbols have been
overlaid to represent a tree and its shadow.
On this pattern a square of light has been
superimposed. The surface light of the
O will be the center of interest in the painting.
The sketch is conforming completely
to the pattern of the structure. All space is positive.

ILLUSTRATION 88-B

SHADOWS—*16″ X 20″*

SHADOWS was painted employing an
underpainting technique. The massive light O
was underpainted in white, the dark O in
tones of blue. The tree was underpainted
white and ochre with the shadows
and windows in pale grey blue.
Ultramarine and umber glazes were painted
in thin passages over all of the cool areas.
Burnt sienna, umber and ochre glazes were laid
over the tree, weeds and wall. The
glazes were lifted from the surface in the
area allotted to the surface light O.
The massive light O in the foundation is still
in light and the structure remains intact.
The surface light O controls the eye movement
and lends a specific mood to the painting.

137

ILLUSTRATION 89-A

DARK DIAGONAL X, *PARALLEL* T *AND* I'S
WITH S *RHYTHM SYMBOL*
AND LANDSCAPE CARTOON OVERLAY

The *X* was placed in a diagonal position
and stretched to the number two, three and four
periphery lines. The top of the dark *X*
meets the dark and light *I*'s and the base of
the dark *T*. The top of the *T* symbol represents
the sky area. The *I*'s and *T* are in a
paralleling pattern but do not overbalance
the diagonal thrust of the *X*.
The *S* symbol was designed over the *X*
to insure control of eye movement and to aid
in the perspective of the landscape. Weeds
and tree motif were designed to correspond to
the pattern of the dark *X* and *T*. The *I*'s
represent rows of grasses and small trees.

ILLUSTRATION 89-B

SPRING THAW—24″ X 36″

This painting was executed employing an acrylic
underpainting. The snow was underpainted
in broad white passages, the weeds and
trees in pale yellow, orange and grey. The sky
carried a tone of light blue.
Ultramarine blue and umber were mixed
to create an oil glaze for the sky. The glaze
was lifted off the sky to establish a cloud
effect. Burnt sienna, umber, and
ochre glazes were brushed over the
grass and tree motif. Accents of ultramarine
blue glazes were added to create a
cold, wet impression in the shadow areas.
The snow pattern was covered with a
thin ocherish glaze and almost completely
removed with cheesecloth. Enough of the glaze
remained to condition the surface
and unify the snow and grass areas. Linear
accents were brushed on the surface to
strengthen the weed and tree motif.

139

5

Introduction to Painting Materials and Terminology

Tʜᴇ ꜰᴏʟʟᴏᴡɪɴɢ sᴇᴄᴛɪᴏɴs are devoted to exercises employing oil as the medium. It is not necessary, however, for the student to work in this medium or limit himself only to oil. Pastel, watercolor or acrylics can be substituted in the color and painting exercises.

PREPARATION OF THE PAINTING SURFACE

The suggested support is ⅛ inch untempered hardboard, such as Masonite or Prestwood, which can be obtained at the local lumber store. The mechanical pattern of the rough side of the board is irritating and unpleasant, so use the smooth side for your painting exercises. This technique of painting relies heavily upon the use of oil glazes which appear best over a completely smooth surface.

There are many brands of acrylic polymer latex base gesso on the market. These products produce a tough, durable and non-absorbent hide that is superior to any other gesso available. Do not use white oil paint for your priming grounds. The oil film resulting will not accept the pastel chalk as readily as a matte gesso surface.

Sand the wooden panel lightly to prepare a soft tooth to insure the best adherence of the gesso to the panel. Thin the gesso in a ratio of ⅔ gesso to ⅓ water before applying it to the surface. Cover the panel with thin coats of paint, each in a different direction, using a soft brush that will not leave brush marks. Let the gesso dry between layers to assure even distribution. Be sure that the dark hardboard color is completely obliterated and the surface smooth. If brush marks appear, sand the surface lightly to relieve it of the irritating pattern.

PREPARATION OF THE PALETTE

Purchase a wooden palette of good size (18″ x 24″) or make one from ¼ inch hardboard or plywood. It is advisable to have a shallow box made with a lid that can be clamped onto it to protect the palette when not in use. Such a box will facilitate transportation and storage of the palette.

Cover the palette surface with several coats of the gesso solution to seal the board and prevent the oil from draining out of the paint. Brush a coat of copal varnish onto the surface to further isolate the ground. Place all of the colors along the periphery of the palette, keeping the transparent and opaque paint separated by the placement of the white. The center of the palette is left vacant for the mixing of paint.

PAINTING ADDITIVES

You will notice that in the suggested supply list I have included Taubes Copal Painting Medium, Taubes Copal Concentrate and Taubes Copal Varnish. These products, the finest on the market, are manufactured by Permanent Pigments of Cincinnati, Ohio. The formulas are those of Frederic Taubes, well known American painter, author and educator.

Taubes Painting Medium Heavy is a solution of linseed oil, turpentine and copal resin. This product facilitates the manipulation and fusion of paint. It will allow the painter to thin the color for transparent films while increasing the brilliance and viscosity. The medium improves the drying properties of the paint, creating a tough, elastic, non-porous paint film.

Taubes Copal Concentrate is a heavy, viscous solution of stand oil and copal resin. Modern pigment is compounded with an additive of aluminum stearate, which accounts for the crisp, short quality of the paint body. The paint in this state is chalky in texture and stubborn in character, making it completely unsatisfactory for the painter. The addition of copal concentrate corrects this condition and renders it LONG. In other words, it changes the texture of the paint to an elastic consistency that will be thoroughly acceptable to the brush. The brilliance and clarity of the color will improve, allowing the painter to utilize the paint to its fullest reflective power.

It has been my experience that most students do not place enough paint on their palettes to complete one painting, much less several. Squeeze at least two inches of each color on the palette. When this has been done, mix a dollop of concentrate about the size of a bean into each mound of paint. The flake white will require twice this amount to render it pliable. When too much concentrate is added, the paint will become enamel-like and unsuitable for general use.

One will observe that a thin skin will form over the mounds of conditioned paint on the palette, while underneath, the paint remains soft and pliable. The palette will stay fresh for many months of painting.

Taubes Copal Varnish is a thin solution suitable for varnishing paintings. It can be used for this purpose after the painting is sufficiently dry (several weeks), to give a low gloss finish that is resistant to dirt.

TOOLS FOR PAINTING

The soft watercolor, flat sabeline brushes are preferable for the application of glazes. This is possibly the most important brush, referred to as a blender. It should be at least ¾ of an inch wide, to permit strong, wide delineations as well as a variety of other effects. All the initial glazes are placed on the painting surface with the blender.

Two sizes of round sable brushes are essential for painting. The sables are conducive to soft paint passages when there is no desire to show heavy impasto. The long-haired scriptliners (commercial lettering brushes) give the painter an implement of remarkable capabilities. These brushes can carry enormous amounts of long, stringy paint that can be drawn over a surface in linear passages. The bristle brushes are energetic tools to be employed when painting heavy impasto and background areas.

PAINTING TERMINOLOGY

A color placed over a canvas or board before the oil passages are applied, is called a GROUND. The employment of a ground color before a painting is begun has long been established as a legitimate procedure of painting. Although this practice was abandoned by the Impressionists (accounting for its neglect in our century), the fact remains obvious that some kind of stain or colored paint layer in the understructure is of tremendous value in achieving effectual painting.

I have chosen the pastel chalk as the ground medium for gaining the underlying color effects throughout these color exercises because the chalk is highly adaptable to the gesso surface, allowing the board to retain the required smooth surface. The transparent nature of the pastels, although flat in appearance, will still allow the luminosity of the gesso priming to reflect through the color. The chalk is adhered to the board with a fixative (hair spray) which dries in a few seconds.

The chalk or ground is held in an understatement of the final intended color. In other words, the chalk color serves as a middle tone. The painter need only paint the dark and light passages, allowing the underlying chalk passages to carry the middle ground colors. This also lends a feeling of continuity and spontaneity to the work.

Oil paint is characterized by two types of paint, transparent and opaque. Transparent paint which has been diluted with Taubes Copal Painting Medium can be laid over the surface with the blender brush in a thin film called a GLAZE. These dark colors are used to their best advantage when painted in veil-like passages over smooth, light colored grounds. This gives the paint added dimension and creates brilliant effects. A white gesso priming on a painting surface acts as the light source, reflecting through the ground color and the transparent paint layer. This luminosity is lost when the transparent color is used with heavy impasto.

When white or opaque paint is added to a glazing color, the color relinquishes its inherent transparent quality and joins the rank and file of the ordinary. This is not to say that they are useless to the painter. On the contrary, the resulting color, though no longer transparent, can function as enticing and valuable opaque scumbles.

The term SCUMBLE refers to the opaque or semi-opaque paint applied over and into wet glazes with brush or knife. Since endless variations of opaque paint can be achieved by mixing any transparent or opaque with another, only a few colors need be considered for the palette.

THE PALETTE

The suggested palette is limited to color of the lightest hues and those with the strongest tinting power. These are easily made darker or weaker by the addition of other paint. You may have already established a preference for certain colors since there are many hundreds of colors available. The colors I recommend are based on a knowledge of their general usefulness.

TRANSPARENT PAINTS

SAP GREEN (Winsor-Newton) is a weak, transparent green *glaze* that mixes well with other colors. This soft green can be painted in thin films to depict leaves and stems, trees, shrubs, grass and cloth. The chalk ground should be kept in various tones of yellow for the best results. You can paint transparent glass vases with this glaze by washing it over grey or yellow grounds. Modify this color with flake white and ochre and it will change to a light yellowish green which will be useful to you when painting opaque leaf forms. You can also employ this same mixture for a neutral background color.

PHTHALOCYANINE GREEN, *glaze,* sports a hue of great brilliance and intensity. It can be extremely effective when producing the illusion of glass. Grey, yellow, blue and green chalk grounds can be placed underneath. If you mix this glaze with phthalocyanine blue, you can achieve a vibrant turquoise. Both of these colors tend to dominate the painting surface if they are used in excess because of their great tinting quality.

ULTRAMARINE BLUE is a *glaze* of purplish hue. When you mix this blue with alizarine crimson, you can achieve fuchsia glazes. Modify ultramarine blue with white and the resulting cool color is pleasant in backgrounds. The coolness of the hue is often complimentary to the hot floral colors. This color can also be of value when painting cloth and ceramic containers. Mixed with ochre, umber and white, beautiful flesh tones are acquired.

PRUSSIAN BLUE is a strong *glaze* which is slightly obnoxious when used in its pure state. When you mix this color with burnt sienna or burnt umber, however, the change in its personality is remarkable. These combinations will provide you with a series of dark green glazes which can be of inestimable value when painting leaves, stems, cloth, transparent glass, silver and pottery vases, rocks, buildings, trees and grass. The chalk ground can extend in range from grey to strong yellow under foliage, grass and water; the blue or grey chalk color under clear glass and white cloth.

PHTHALOCYANINE BLUE is a sweet blue *glazing* color of great brilliance. You can paint transparent containers with this color, relying on variation of pink, blue and grey chalk in the ground color for the subtle changes that appear in the top layer of paint. Combine this color with flake white and it becomes a pleasant blue opaque that is suitable for backgrounds, cloth and ceramic pottery.

BURNT SIENNA is a *glaze* of exceptional beauty. Its fiery red color enhances the aesthetic enjoyment of many a painting. A glaze of burnt sienna will produce the color seen in the centers and hollows of marigolds, zinnias, sunflowers and black-eyed susans. When you are painting dried leaf and flower forms, this is certainly the color to choose. The chalk ground can be pink, green or yellow under the red-brown leaves.

Burnt sienna is the color to use when you are depicting amber glass, copper or brass containers. The most brilliant effects can be achieved by keeping the chalk ground color in tones of yellow. Pink and green grounds can be effective when painting corroded copper cauldrons. It also produces a lively wood effect when depicting tables or floors or painting clay pots and brick walls.

As a landscape color, it is invaluable for grasses, tree trunks, buildings and rocks. Burnt sienna is also a useful color as a glaze over flesh tones. When you wish to paint red hair, use a yellow ground and glaze the hair area with this color.

BURNT UMBER, a dark, rich brown, is a *glaze* that you can employ to paint weed, glass, leaf, copper, brass and ceramic pottery. When mixed with Prussian blue, a glaze of greyish-green results, which can be effective when painting a clear glass vase. Achieve the shadow area of white cloth by using this glaze followed by white scumbles. This mixture has a subtle dark look to it which makes it representative of cast and natural shadow. Chalk grounds of orange, pink, yellow and green are pleasing under the brown glaze.

Again, this glaze is beautiful when painting rocks, grasses, buildings, etc. It is a color useful to the portrait painter as a shadow glaze or as an additive to cool ochre or orange in depicting flesh. Umber will cool and grey any color. Burnt umber can be used in the pure glaze state for painting brown hair. When ultramarine is added, the transparent mixture turns dark and can resemble brown and black hair, depending upon your choice of the tonal value of the chalk ground underneath.

ALIZARINE CRIMSON is a brilliant red *glaze,* absolutely necessary when painting flowers. Glaze over pink and orange chalk ground with this magnificent color to gain the illusion of flowers and cloth. You can heighten the color and make it even more intense by glazing over yellow chalk grounds. A blue chalk ground with alizarine crimson glaze painted over it can result in rich purple and fuchsia color films. When you have occasion to paint ruby glass, glaze with alizarine crimson and darken the shadow with ultramarine blue. Select a pink or grey chalk ground when seeking a transparent, silky red effect of a tablecloth or scarf. Alizarine mixed with white is unpleasant and of little or no value but a passage of cadmium red scumbled into alizarine crimson will give the impression of light striking a flower petal or fold of a cloth. Alizarine crimson will improve in texture if the oil in the paint is drained from it and replaced with an addition of copal concentrate.

ROSE RED (Shiva) is another brilliant red *glaze,* similar but lighter in hue than alizarine crimson. If you modify this color with white, you can create a beautiful rose color. This is the only true pink on the palette. All other pinks are achieved by glazing over pink chalk grounds with alizarine crimson or rose red.

IVORY BLACK, *glaze,* is most helpful in painting the still life accessories. Depict iron kettles or pots by glazing ivory black over blue, grey or red chalk grounds. It can be used for the shadow area of copper, brass, silver and ceramic containers. Ivory black blends well into the painting surface because of its extremely weak tinting power. Most of your black effects can be made with a combination of ultramarine blue and umber. When mixed with yellows, it renders a beautiful green. This glazing color is suitable in landscape for weeds, grasses, buildings and rocks.

OPAQUE PAINTS

FLAKE WHITE is a very dense, *opaque* white which is superior to the other white paint on the market. The most charming attribute of flake white is its ability to render itself long when mixed with copal concentrate. The term LONG refers to the stringy quality of the paint after a large addition of copal concentrate has been blended into it and the mixture is allowed to stand a few days. This enables the painter to use his brush and paint very much as he would with a pencil. The flake white paint can be combined with any color on the palette to achieve delicate pastel shades of linear paint. A scriptliner brush filled with this paint can be strung over the surface, depositing the color in thin, raised lines, such as the tracing of delicate patterns of a lace or fringed table-cloth. A dot of such paint can effectively indicate a highlight on a pottery or glass vase.

THALO YELLOW GREEN (Grumbacher) is a light, spring green *opaque* color which is delightful when used by itself or mixed with ochre or flake white. If this color is thinned with painting medium, you can apply it in a semi-transparent manner over yellow or grey chalk grounds to achieve the effect of tender, young growth in still life and landscape painting. Thalo yellow green is an especially complimentary background color when cut with white.

HANSA YELLOW LIGHT is a strong, bright yellow *opaque,* much superior to and easier to control than cadmium yellow light. This color can be thinned with painting medium and used as a glaze if the chalk ground remains in pale yellow or white. The ground color must be lighter than the paint to achieve a transparent effect. If you mix Hansa yellow light with burnt umber, the result will be a beautiful olive-green. Mix Hansa with cadmium orange or cadmium red and you extend this into a great variety of additional colors. It is extremely useful for opaque passages on fruit, foliage, flowers, fields and cloth.

YELLOW OCHRE is an *opaque* dull earth-yellow of great versatility. When you mix this color with the blues and greens on the palette, you can gain many new hues. Ochre, placed in juxtaposition with cadmium red, will assume a green appearance which can lend enchanting effects. Ochre can easily be rendered long with further addition of copal concentrate, creating paint suitable for linear passages. It can also be thinned with painting medium and laid over the painting surface to achieve semi-transparent glazes. When you use it in this manner, your ground color will be green, yellow or grey. Ochre is a beautiful opaque landscape color used to portray water, grasses, trees, rocks and buildings. It is equally important when you are painting golden flesh tones.

CADMIUM ORANGE LIGHT, *opaque,* is quite necessary to have on the palette when painting floral motifs. This color is a strong, clear orange which has a flower-like quality in itself. When you mix it with cadmium red light and Hansa yellow light, you extend the color range for scumbling. Cadmium orange can be painted in veil-like films, much as you would a true glaze, if it is thinned well with painting medium. Keep the chalk ground color in shades of yellow, pink and orange for the best results. It has extensive use in depicting cloth and background.

CADMIUM RED LIGHT, *opaque,* is a bright red which resembles vermillion and can serve as a transparent color when it is thinned with medium and applied over light chalk grounds of pink and orange. It does not mix well with white: the resulting mixture is wishy-washy and of little value. Mix this color with alizarine crimson, however, and the result will be a large range of beautiful dark reds, desirable for flower scumbles. This eliminates the need for the dark and medium cadmium reds on the palette. Due to the wood-like feeling of cadmium red light, it can be used to simulate wood surfaces. Try it also when you are painting clay pottery, using Venetian red to represent the shadowed side of the flower pot. The effect will be rewarding. Keep the chalk grounds pink, red, orange or yellow under both wood and pottery.

VENETIAN RED, sometimes called *Light Red,* is a dull, *opaque* color. It is extremely valuable when painting pottery, wood, cloth and brick. Due to its strong tinting ability, it should be used with discretion. Venetian red often compliments the brilliant glazes because of its strong opaque quality.

This color can be used in mixture with umber and ochre for the pink tone in flesh. It is also a beautiful scumble when depicting red earth in landscape painting.

LIST OF MATERIALS

1. Easel
2. Hardboard cut into these suggested sizes: 5x7, 8x10, 9x12, 11x14, 16x20, 12x24, 18x24, 15x30
3. One pint of Acrylic Polymer Latex Base Gesso
4. One pint of Acrylic Polymer Latex Base Modeling Paste
5. Palette (18x24)
6. Oil Paints: Sap Green (Winsor-Newton), Phthalocyanine Green, Ultramarine Blue, Prussian Blue, Burnt Sienna, Phthalocyanine Blue, Burnt Umber, Alizarine Crimson, Rose Red (Shiva), Ivory Black, Flake White, "Thalo" Yellow Green (Grumbacher), Hansa Yellow Light, Yellow Ochre, Cadmium Red Light, Venetian Red
7. Taubes Copal Painting Medium, heavy or light
8. Taubes Copal Concentrate
9. Taubes Copal Varnish
10. Oil Cups
11. Brushes: one ¾″ flat blender, one flat sable #12, one round sable #6, one round sable #12, one scriptliner #1 (Delta pure red sable), one scriptliner #3, one scriptliner #6, one bristle brush #6 or 7, one bristle brush #10 or 11
12. Small box of pastel chalk
13. Pencils and charcoal (vine)
14. Fixative (hair spray without lanolin)
15. Several sheets of tracing paper
16. One sheet of graphite paper
17. Small squares of cheesecloth

6

Introduction to Color

EXPERIMENTS
1. TRANSPARENT COLOR
2. MIXING TRANSPARENT COLOR
3. OPAQUE COLOR
4. MIXING TRANSPARENT AND OPAQUE COLOR

Materials:
Four 18″x24″ pressed wood panels prepared as directed
The palette set up as directed
Pastel chalks
Hair spray (without lanolin)
Taubes Copal Painting Medium
Brushes

IDENTIFICATION OF COLOR

THE APPLICATION OF COLOR is the student's entrance into the world of the painter. An ability to disperse this pigment over a surface in an intriguing manner is termed talent, but not necessarily intuitive insight. The student who seems deficient in this ability is more often inhibited by lack of basic color principles than he is by inferior talent.

Color is pigment measured by its reflective power which determines its hue and intensity by registering its reflection on the retina. Such registration results in a human reaction; consequently, the painter, aware of visual sensation, can regulate the impact of his painting. Such color knowledge can only be learned through practical application and experimentation.

COLOR DEPTH

In the previous section you have been dealing with two-dimension movement (black and white) on a two-dimensional surface. As soon as color is introduced, the complexity of the compositional problems emerges. Color moves in depth. The cool range of color which consists of blue, green and white recedes from the picture plane. The hot colors, red, orange, and yellow, move forward. You are now not only considering line, shape and structure but the advancement and recession of color in space. The warm and cool color movement is a "constant" principle of sound composition.

An addition of white to any color mutes it and moves it into the depth of the painting. Blue is a more recessive color than green and green can be brought forward with the addition of yellow. Red is the most dominant color in the spectrum; all the colors in the hot range take second seat to it. This means that yellow moves back from red, yet still remains on the front of the surface plane. For instance, if cadmium red light is placed in juxtaposition with ochre, the yellow color will assume a cool role and appear green.

It is absolutely necessary to acquaint yourself with color and its intrinsic nature in order to understand the possibilities to which it can best be utilized. Each color has an identity, displaying idiosyncrasies of its own and personality changes when in mixture or in juxtaposition with each other.

EXPERIMENTING WITH COLOR

The way to gain color understanding is to experiment with a spectrum of pigment individually. It is my suggestion that you set up a program of study through the use of color charts, using oil as the medium. In an effort to simplify the course of study, I have organized the exercises into four color chart experiments.

You will first investigate a small range of transparent colors by placing them over various colored grounds. You then will experiment by mixing one transparent color with another to enable you to extend your palette without adding additional color. The third exercise is intended to acquaint you with opaque paint and the influence of one color on another. The last color chart explains the mixing of glazes and opaques together and the mixing of one opaque with another opaque.

EXPERIMENTING WITH TRANSPARENT COLOR

You will experiment only with transparent color in the exercise. Prepare your chart by dividing it into six sections and rubbing pastel chalk on the surface as diagrammed. Use hair spray to fix the chalk to the board. Follow the palette outline and lay brush-width thin, transparent washes over the various pastel chalk passages. Begin at the left and continue through the panel in one movement. Keep a record of the transparent oil color so you can refer to your chart in the future. Note the change of effects as the various colors pass over the different chalk colors. You can see immediately the endless possibilities for application.

EXPERIMENTING WITH MIXING TRANSPARENT COLOR

Prepare this chart exactly as you did the first. Refer to the information given in the palette introduction for mixtures of transparent color. See Section V.

EXPERIMENTING WITH OPAQUE COLOR

Prepare this chart in the same manner as the first two. Place the pastel on the board and fix it. Refer to your palette information and experiment with all of the opaque colors by placing them over the chalk ground. You are observing the juxtaposition of color.

EXPERIMENTING WITH MIXING TRANSPARENT AND OPAQUE COLOR

Prepare the chart as before. Begin by placing a transparent wash over the pastel as you did in the first chart. Now, using a bristle brush, place opaque color into the thin transparent paint layers. Mix two opaques together and repeat the exercise. Mix an opaque with a transparent color. The transparent color loses its identity but becomes a new opaque color for your palette.

Opaque paint

Transparent paint

ILLUSTRATION 90

PALETTE SET-UP

ILLUSTRATION 91

COLOR CHART DIAGRAM

Divide a panel (18″ x 24″) in six vertical sections.
Rub pastel chalk into the designated areas:

WHITE	PINK	YELLOW	ORANGE	BLUE	GREEN

ILLUSTRATION 92

COLOR CHART

The panel was prepared in the manner described and divided into six sections—each section carrying a different colored chalk. This illustration explains the first exercise in experimenting with color. Only the transparent color has been employed. Note the influence of the chalk color underneath the color film.

Colors used:
Sap green
Phthalocyanine green
Phthalocyanine blue
Ultramarine blue
Burnt sienna
Burnt umber
Ivory black
Alizarine crimson
Rose red

7

Application of Color

COLOR IN RHYTHM

Presuming you now have some knowledge of the characteristics of color, it is time to use it. This section is devoted to color exercises which enable you to put your color knowledge into a working situation. Your first experiment is with color in rhythm, employing the curved letter symbols to control the two dimensional surface movement.

EXPERIMENTING WITH COLOR IN RHYTHM

The key word is *rhythm*. Move it, weave it, but *control* it! Select a board that has been prepared as instructed in the preceding section. Cover the total surface with an ochre colored chalk ground. Fix the chalk to the board with hair spray. Choose three transparent colors, one warm and two cool. Begin with the warm color at the focal point area and, painting the color in pieces and shapes rather than in a continuous line, move it over the surface in an *S* movement. Do not try to move it with a specific motif. Keep the shapes abstract and with no objective but to experience the color shapes in the dimensional movement. Now add the cool colors one at a time, beginning at a different point on the surface. Paint them in another *S* movement by weaving the colors over the surface.

Try various color combinations, changing the ground color as well as the oil glazes. Use the curved letter symbols explained in Section IV to increase the experimental value and stimulate the exercises. Fill the total space, eliminating all the ground color. Avoid monotonous shapes by being conscious of the shapes you are forming as well as the movement of color. Be aware of juxtaposition of color within the forms. By placing different pressure on the brush and by overlaying color, seek tone value relationships. A square of cheesecloth (4"x4") wrapped about the finger is used to relieve the glazes, exposing the chalk grounds underneath.

COLOR IN STRUCTURE

The second group of exercises is directed to the movements of color in three dimensional depth in combination with a solid structure idea, utilizing the straight letter symbols. You will also be introduced to textures that create a surface pattern.

EXPERIMENTING WITH COLOR IN STRUCTURE

Select a white gesso board and cover the surface with a layer of ocherish colored chalk. Choose a structural pattern from the straight letter symbols that conform to the size of your painting surface. Consider only structure and not a pictorial motif. Transfer the outline of the pattern to the board with graphite paper. Choose two transparent colors, one cool and one warm. Use your blending brush and paint the warm color in the dark areas of the structure and the cool colors in the light areas. Seek color modulation by lifting the glazes from the surface with cheesecloth and by over-laying one glaze passage with another. Select another board and two warm transparent colors; use a cool ground and repeat the exercise with a different structural pattern. Repeat again, selecting a warm chalk ground and painting with two cool transparent colors.

EXPERIMENTING WITH COLOR
IN STRUCTURE AND TEXTURE

Use your modeling paste and stipple a textural relief over the area confined to the dark structural pattern only. This surface must be allowed to dry 24 hours. The modeling paste may have formed cracks in the surface. If this occurs, fill them with an addition of paste and let the surface dry for another 24 hours.

Texture can serve as a useful tool supporting your structure and adding surface interest. It should be used only in places as an intentional accent.

You may now change your chalk ground to two colors, one for the light pattern and one for the dark. Proceed as before with a limited oil palette, experimenting over and over again with various combinations of structural patterns, textured areas and color schemes.

93-A—MULTIPLE S SYMBOLS IN COMBINATION

The diagram explains the directional pattern of four S symbols
employing two cool colors and two warm colors. Your experiments
should encompass many variations of both the S and C
symbols with warm and cool colors employed in juxtaposition.
Such experiments will increase your awareness of
color movement both in two dimension and in depth.

94-A—DARK X AND I IN COMBINATION

The structure pattern was designed to guide you into experiencing
color in depth with direct application of straight line symbols.
Experiment with many structural patterns holding the warm color in
the dark and the cool colors in the light structure pattern.
Reverse the procedure by painting the cool color in the dark and
the warm in the light.

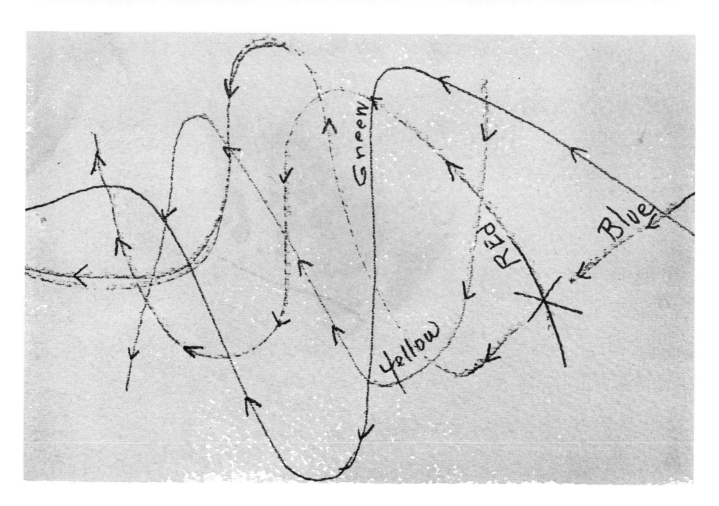

93-B—FLORAL DESIGN CREATED BY THE APPLICATION OF FOUR S SYMBOLS

The illustration is the result of an experiment in color movement.
There was no initial intent to create a floral motif; however,
once the procedure was begun the placement of color began to assume
the identity of flowers.
Alizarine crimson glazes (a definite floral color) were placed in the
focal point area and moved through the surface in an S rhythm.
A Hansa yellow pattern was then established by using another
S movement, sap green glazes assumed still another S rhythm and were
followed by ultramarine blue. The background area was
relieved of the glaze to emphasize the floral suggestion.

94-B—LANDSCAPE DESIGN CREATED BY THE APPLICATION OF THE X AND I SYMBOLS

Hot burnt sienna and umber glazes were painted into the dark X
and I structure pattern with no intent to establish a subject idea.
Ultramarine glazes were painted in thin washes in the light I pattern of
the structure. Sap green glazes were painted into the
remaining light pattern. The relationship of color began to
suggest trees, rocks, sky and water. The glazes were relieved and linear
accents were added to emphasize the suggested motif.

ILLUSTRATION 95

TEXTURE

A detail of the painting GOLDEN AGE
has been reproduced here to explain the use of
modeling paste when textural effects
are desired on a surface of a painting. In the
early stages of this painting modeling paste
was stippled into the light areas of the
tree stumps. A wood texture was desired to give
the painting interest and to promote eye
movement through the surface. The
painting was executed on canvas employing
an underpainting technique.
The tree stumps were underpainted in
tones of ochre, pink and orange. Once the acrylic
underpainting and the textural pattern created
by modeling paste was dry, oil glazes
of burnt sienna, umber and Prussian blue
were brushed on the surface. The glazes
were relieved to such a degree as to establish
several color values on the surface of
the painting. Light colored scumbles were
then rapidly applied with a knife
over the rough surface to add still another
dimension to the motif.
The background was underpainted in Venetian
red. Gold leaf was then glued to the
surface with varnish and antiqued with burnt
umber and ivory black glazes. The gold
metallic background lends a
highly decorative quality to the work.

8

Painting the Picture

EXPERIMENT
APPLICATION OF ALL PRINCIPLES OF COMPOSITION

THE LAST GROUP OF EXERCISES encompasses the addition of a motif to the structural and rhythm patterns. You are approaching the business of painting a picture, incorporating all of the knowledge gained through the total compositional study. It is advisable to keep your motif simple: a vase of flowers, a head or a single tree. Remember, these are exercises to teach you composition. Your intent is to select a pictorial theme and house it in an abstract structure. A masterpiece seldom results at this point in your learning.

A FEW WORDS CONCERNING TECHNIQUE

I have selected a simple pastel chalk and oil paint technique for the execution of these exercises. This technique is by no means the only one available to you. There are many sound techniques that could be discussed, but since we are primarily concerned here with the application of compositional principles, it seems inappropriate to go into various techniques. I have selected a procedure that best facilitates the extention of compositional principles with a working situation. I developed this technique several years ago from a working knowledge of classic procedures taught me by Frederic Taubes, the contemporary master and authority on classic procedures. Several paintings are reproduced in this section with explanatory notes on the procedure of execution.

The technique employs the use of pastel chalk as a ground color. This enables you to use this underlying color as a middle tone for your painting. The oil glazes are your dark passages and the opaques are your very light ones. This means that you utilize the pastel chalk in the lower layer as both light and dark middle tone values. Such a procedure will facilitate the rapid execution of a work because you need only consider the very dark and very light paint passages. It also lends a quality of spontaneity to a painting despite the laborious work that has preceded the actual laying on of paint.

EXPERIMENTING WITH ALL PRINCIPLES OF COMPOSITION ON A PAINTING SURFACE

Select a theme for the painting. It is best to make several complete drawings of the idea on transparent transfer paper. Relate the theme to a board size. Now, draw several structural ideas that can be the foundation of your light and dark pattern. Choose the most compatible design to go with the motif by laying the transparent drawing over your light and dark pattern. Make any adjustments necessary to maintain the light and dark pattern and the theme. Check your surface for negative space areas and correct them.

Once you have selected the drawing of the motif and the structural pattern best suited for each other, you can begin. Transfer your drawing of the motif to your painting surface. You may clarify the design by drawing over the surface with pencil or pastel chalk. Fix the drawing with hair spray. Decide on a color scheme and place a pastel chalk ground on the surface. This can be a single color or multicolored, depending upon the motif idea. Keep the chalk grounds light and well-blended. Fix the chalk ground with hair spray. Once the surface is dry, you are ready to proceed in oil.

Use your wide blending brush and apply the transparent paint passages. These dark colors will form the structure. The glazes are lifted in part from the light areas of the structure. The dark glazes are holding the structural form to the periphery edge. At this point you can clearly identify your letter structure on the surface. You can also identify your motif idea which is evident through the transparent glazes.

Your next step is to develop the motif idea by painting additional glazes in the forms created by the drawing of the motif. You are concerned with light and dark modulation of objects within the subject idea itself. Lift areas of glaze from the objects with cheesecloth. You are exposing the colored chalk ground underneath, representing the middle tone value of the object. The remaining glaze encompasses both the middle tone darks and the darkest darks. *Do not allow disintegration of your structure.* The pattern will no longer necessarily be recognizable as letter form but you must hold the light and dark structure over the total surface.

The oil glazes must be allowed to become tacky before you can successfully place the opaques into the wet surface. This means that the turpentine must be given time to evaporate from the medium which was used as a dilutant for the oil glazes. When the glazes are sticky to touch, they will be tough enough to hold the opaque in place. The painting at this point is ready to accept the opaques. Keep the light paint only in the areas intended to carry the very light passages. Do not destroy the beauty of the transparent paint by an overstatement in opaque. Establish the light structural pattern by lifting the glazes to the ground color and by over-laying with light opaque color.

When painting the objects of the motif, you are considering only the objects on the front plane of the surface; that is, the objects and color that are moving toward you.

Paint the opaques only into the areas reserved for the very light. Don't destroy your middle tone values that have been established by the chalk grounds.

The success of the finished product depends upon your ability to apply all of the principles of good composition in combination with your skill and, of course, innate talent. Illusive? Yes. But now you have a foundation of knowledge; a program that enables you to discipline your talent. What you do with the knowledge, discipline and talent is completely up to you.

ILLUSTRATION 96-A

*PARALLEL DARK AND LIGHT I'S
AND SURFACE LIGHT O
WITH PORTRAIT CARTOON OVERLAY*

The dark and light *I*'s were stretched vertically through the surface and a cartoon for PORTRAIT OF LISA overlaid. The dark *I* is conforming to the center axis line of the head while the surface *O* is conforming to the side plane of the face. The remaining light pattern can be seen as middle tone value. The structure and subject are compatible. The structure can be held intact by adapting a lighting pattern for the head that corresponds with the dark and light structure. A simple division down the center of the front facial plane places the left side in dark and the right side in light.

96-B—*PASTEL CHALK UNDERPAINTING FOR* PORTRAIT OF LISA

This illustration explains the second step in the technique recommended for the painting exercises. An 8″ x 10″ gessoed board was selected and a drawing made of the model. The drawing was transferred to the board with graphite paper. The lines were reestablished with pencil and adhered to the support with hair spray. Orange pastel chalk was then rubbed into the hair and light side of the face. A lime green chalk was selected for the costume, pink for the background. A blue chalk was rubbed into the area reserved for the dark *I* of the structure. The same color corresponds to the dark side of the face. Additional blue chalk was rubbed across the bridge of the nose and through the eye area to accommodate the dark color of the eyes of the model. The chalk ground was then fixed to the board with hair spray.

96-C—PORTRAIT OF LISA—*8″ X 10″*

Ultramarine blue, burnt umber, ochre and white oil paints were mixed together to create a semi-glaze. This mixture was brushed over the flesh area in a thin passage, using the flat blender brush with the copal painting medium as a dilutant. A pure glaze of burnt umber was used to achieve the very dark strands of hair. The structure was emphasized with a glaze of umber and ultramarine blue. A sap green glaze was brushed over the dress and an alizarine crimson glaze was placed over the light structure area. The glazes that covered the total surface were allowed to become tacky. Cheesecloth was used to lift the glaze from the light side of the face, hair and costume to establish a middle tone value. The dark eyes were painted with a #4 bristle brush, using a glaze of umber and ultramarine. The same mixture, with a small addition of ochre and white, was used to paint the opaque scumbles around the eyes, under the nose, onto the lips and under the chin. In this painting, there was no apparent need to . paint light opaque passages. The white from the gesso surface is conveyed through the pastel chalk and top glaze, giving an illusion of young, vibrant flesh. The pencil drawing and pastel chalk ground can be identified on the finished surface, lending a sense of animation to the finished work. A scriptliner brush was used to delineate the accents in the hair, eyelids, nose and mouth. The process from the drawing to the full color painting was completed within a thirty minute period, substantiating the spontaneous quality of the painting.

ILLUSTRATION 97-A

DARK L *AND LIGHT* O
WITH LANDSCAPE CARTOON OVERLAY

A dark parallel *L* was stretched through
the surface to meet all four periphery edges.
A cartoon of trees, rocks and horses was
drawn on transfer paper and laid over the
structure. The motif was organized to correspond
exactly with the underlying structure.

97-B—*PASTEL CHALK UNDERPAINTING FOR* HORSES IN LANDSCAPE

The drawing was transferred to gesso board and reestablished with
additional pencil drawing. Pink, yellow-green and brown chalk
were then rubbed on the surface and fixed. The colors were intentionally
applied in a haphazard manner to aid an open color technique
intended for the final oil painting. *Open color is a painting term
implying the continuous movement of color from one
object to another with only a line denoting a change of form.*

97-C—HORSES IN LANDSCAPE—9½″ X 18″

Warm glazing colors were brushed over the total painting surface.
Ochre, cadmium red and Hansa yellow were thinned
with copal painting medium and used as glazes along with ultramarine
blue, burnt umber and burnt sienna. The ivory black glaze
in the tree and horse located on the right of the surface has assumed
a cool green attitude because of its juxtaposition with the bright
Hansa yellow. The black also aids in the loose interpretation
of the dark *L* structure. Burnt umber glazes were painted in the
foreground and move through the horses and trees at the left,
further identifying the dark structure force. The glazes were allowed to
stand on the surface until they became tacky. A portion
of the glazes was then lifted from the surface in the light forms of
the trees and horses, exposing the multicolored chalk ground.
Orange and yellow scumbles were brushed quickly into the sky using
a wide bristle brush. Small opaque areas were painted
into the light planes of the horses and into the hills. Ivory black linear
accents were added with a #1 scriptliner brush. The entire
painting was executed in a matter of minutes
which added to the fluid appearance of the painting.

ILLUSTRATION 98-A

*PARALLEL LIGHT AND DARK L'S
WITH BUILDING CARTOON OVERLAY*

Two light *L*'s and one dark *L* were placed
in a parallel horizontal position in a
vertical shape. A cartoon of a building idea was
placed over the structure. Diagonal lines
have been drawn into the cartoon
to explain the motif idea. They are not, however,
interfering with the parallel structure
built with the *L* symbols.

173

ILLUSTRATION 98-B AND 98-C

98-B—*PASTEL CHALK UNDERPAINTING FOR* ROOFTOPS

A sepia colored chalk was used to establish the drawing
on the white gessoed panel. The drawing was fixed with hair spray.
Yellow and orange chalks were then rubbed lightly over the white
walls; blue and umber chalks were used to establish the dark structure
pattern. The chalk was then adhered to the surface with hair spray.

98-C—ROOFTOPS—*15″ X 30″*

Hansa yellow and cadmium orange were thinned to a glazing
consistency and washed over the rooftops and chimneys. The color was
allowed to move outside of the contour line in order to
facilitate the use of open color.
Umber, ultramarine blue and ochre glazes were brushed into
the dark structure pattern. The glazes were allowed to reach
a tacky stage before a portion of the paint was lifted off to expose the
chalk underpainting and establish the middle tone value.
Dark accents, both opaque and linear, were painted into the
window areas. Opaque passages were brushed on the sides of the
buildings and pale orange and yellow opaque added to the rooftops.
The painting, although quite a good size, was executed in
one sitting. The open color lends an abstract quality to the already
translucent paint quality. The chalk drawing can be identified
through the paint films lending a sketchy, spontaneous look to the work.

ILLUSTRATION 99-A

*PARALLEL DARK AND LIGHT I'S
WITH LANDSCAPE
AND BARN CARTOON OVERLAY*

This simple *I* structure was designed to
house a landscape and building motif.
The *I*'s were placed in both horizontal and
vertical positions in a narrow horizontal shape.
The vertical *I*'s represent light and dark
tree forms while the horizontal *I*'s
identify a pattern for a striped field motif.
The barn was simply superimposed over
the center of the structure. The *I*'s hold the dark
mass in position. The barn, although somewhat
nostalgic, has been reduced to a classic
building shape. All unnecessary accompaniment,
such as windmills and fences
have been eliminated to prevent its
classification as an illustrative subject.

ILLUSTRATIONS 99-B AND 99-C

99-B—*PASTEL CHALK UNDERPAINTING FOR* THE BARN

The cartoon for the painting was transferred to a white panel
and the drawing reestablished with pencil. Orange and yellow chalk
passages were rubbed on the surface in the tree and grass areas.
The barn was covered with a blue chalk and the entire surface
fixed with hair spray.

99-C—THE BARN—*8″ X 16″*

Burnt sienna and umber oil glazes were brushed into the trees
and grass areas. Hansa yellow was thinned to a glazing consistency and
washed over the remaining light pattern. Ultramarine blue and
umber were mixed and placed over the total building.
When the glazes became tacky the middle tone values were established
by lifting off the glazes and exposing the chalk ground. Linear
accents were brushed into the trees, grasses and barn.
Hansa yellow and white were mixed and flicked into the wet glazes
to establish the detail pattern of the grass. A #1 scriptliner
was used to paint the light stems. A few opaque grey
passages were added to the barn structure. The majority of the surface
is transparent with the opaques held to an absolute minimum.
The total effect is fluid and translucent.

ILLUSTRATION 100-A

SINGLE DARK X
WITH FIGURE CARTOON OVERLAY

A dark X pattern was stretched through
the total space in a parallel position. The cartoon
of a mother and child was placed
over the structure. The execution of the motif
demands a further commitment to light
areas within the massive dark structure force. The
dark X must be retained to the degree that
it extends to the periphery lines
and securely holds the figures in position.

100-B—*TONED GROUND FOR* MOTHER AND CHILD

The support now is a toned ground canvas. This illustration
has been included to explain the painting procedure used in some
of the illustrations in Section IV. The canvas was primed
with several coats of white acrylic gesso just as it comes from the
container. Each application was allowed to dry thoroughly.
The surface was sanded between each application to insure a smooth
painting surface. The final priming was a pale pink
achieved by the mixing of cadmium red acrylic with gesso.
A cartoon for the painting was then drawn directly on to the canvas
and fixed with hair spray. The toned ground serves
as a middle tone color for the dark and light oil paint.

100-C—MOTHER AND CHILD—*18″ X 24″*

Burnt sienna oil glazes were brushed over the total surface and lifted off
in the background and the planes of the figures (conforming
to the left light direction). Ochre was thinned to a glazing consistency
and brushed into the light areas of the figures. Burnt umber glazes
were used to deepen the dark shadow. Ultramarine blue
and umber were mixed together and brushed into the costume.
The glazes were allowed to become tacky and the light areas
were again cleared of glazes, exposing the pink toned ground which is
serving as a middle tone value. Pale pink opaques
were brushed into the background and along the left side of figures.
The structure was maintained by allowing the dark glazes
to surround the figures and connect to the periphery edge. The
pink ground of the painting is identifiable under the
transparent paint film and in many areas left completely free of paint.

ILLUSTRATION 101-A

PARALLEL DARK H *AND* I
WITH S *AND* C *RHYTHM SYMBOLS*
AND STILL LIFE CARTOON OVERLAY

The dark distorted *H* was stretched in an upright
position through the lower three-fourths
of the painting surface converging on the
numbers two, three and four periphery lines.
A dark *I* was placed in a horizontal
position on the number one line.
The cartoon for the painting was laid over the
structure and the objects drawn to conform to
the dark *H* of the structure. The watermelon is
acting as the focal point because of its
position and color intent. The rhythm is continued
by additional *C* and *S* symbols. The objects
are held together by the dark shadow
pattern on the table.

ILLUSTRATIONS 101-B AND 101-C

101-B—*UNDERPAINTING FOR* STILL LIFE WITH FRUIT

This painting has been included to explain the technique
of acrylic underpainting. The canvas surface received several layers of
white gesso priming and was kept smooth by sanding
between layers. The last priming coat was tinted blue. Pale acrylic colors
were then painted into the areas intended to house the still life objects
—pink under red, yellow under green and yellow, pale orange
under orange, white under white and grey under blue.
All detail of the objects was eliminated and the painting held in
a complete understatement.

101-C—STILL LIFE WITH FRUIT—*30″ X 40″*

The underpainting surface was first sanded and a coat of
painting medium applied. Transparent paint was brushed on the
surface, corresponding to the color present in the underpainting.
Alizarine crimson was painted over the pink areas, Hansa yellow over
the yellow, sap green over the yellow leaves and the green
color of the fruit. Cadmium orange was brushed over the pale orange
in the orange flowers and fruit. Ultramarine and umber
glazes were brushed into the background and shadow patterns
created by the objects. The glazes were allowed to become tacky and
were then lifted off in the middle ground areas.
Opaque lights were scumbled freely over the light patterns
of the fruit, flowers and table. A burnt sienna drawing was incorporated
at this point maintaining the open color feeling of the objects. The
transparent color and the free brush strokes lend a
watercolor feeling to the total work.

9

Glossary and Composition Checkpoints

GLOSSARY

abstract: a distortion of form

attitude: the essence of an expression

background: area surrounding objects of a motif

cartoon: a rough sketch of a painting in the preparatory stage

chiaroscuro: a painting or drawing using only light and shade

classic: traditional; of the highest excellence

classic lighting: light directed from any one side of an object

color: the visual impact of the reflection of pigment on the retina of the eye

composition: line, form, balance, color, rhythm, space — a theme housed in an abstract structure

concentrate: a liquid used to render oil paints to an elastic consistency

contour line: that line which defines the shape of an object

cool colors: consisting of the blues, greens and white

curved letter symbols: *S* and *C*—used to create rhythm in a painting

fixative: hair spray — a solution sprayed on drawings to prevent smudging

focal point: the entrance and exit necessary for the visual enjoyment of a painting

form: the enclosed shape of an object or space

gesso: an acrylic polymer latex base — used as a priming agent for painting surfaces

gesture line: a free, loose line defining an attitude or movement

glaze: a transparent film of paint

hue: a tint or shade of color

impasto: the laying on of paint thickly

lifting off (relief of glazes): a technique; using cheesecloth to remove paint (glazes) to reveal underpainting and/or toned ground

line: a tool used by an artist to denote form and emotion

long paint: a consistency created by mixing oil paint and copal concentrate; an elastic, enamel-like paint

middle ground: the area between the foreground and horizon of a landscape painting

middle tone: the tonal value between highlight and dark of a painting

motif: the theme or subject idea for a painting

negative space: any space which is not enclosed by line, texture, or color

opaque: paint which is not transparent

painting medium: a liquid composition containing copal resin used to improve the viscosity of oil paint; a dilutant for paint

passages: brush strokes

periphery: the outermost edge of a form (the boundary edges of the canvas)

picture plane: the surface of the canvas; an area of a two dimensional surface

point of interest: the main idea or object of the motif

positive space: enclosed space (by line, texture or color)

priming: preparing the surface of a canvas or board for paint with a solution such as gesso and water

rhythm symbols: S and C — used to create rhythm in a painting

sabeline: a synthetic material used in brushes in place of sable

scumbles: passages of opaque paint applied with brush or knife

static: a line or shape which has little or no emotional character

straight letter symbols: X, I, Y, L, T, H and O (squared, $\square$); those letters used to design abstract structures for a painting

structure: the foundation of a composition created by the adaptation of straight letter symbols to create balance by the dispersion of light and shade

structure symbols: straight letter symbols; a symbol used to create an abstract form to structure a painting

symbolism: a system of symbols; the use of letters to form structure

tacky: a sticky condition on a glazed painting surface which makes it acceptable to opaque scumbles

technique: a methodical process to bring about a finished painting; the use of different methods or materials to paint a picture

theme: a motif; a subject idea

three dimensional: moving in depth as well as width and height

tonal value: an overall color of a painting, also toned ground color

transparent paint: as opposed to opaque paint; a paint applied to the canvas in thin, film-like glazes allowing drawing and/or color underneath to be seen

two dimensional: moving in width and height only; having elements organized in a flat surface

underpaint: to paint or color with a medium like or different from the medium used to complete a painting. To prepare a picture with color other than the finishing paint to create a middle tone

understatement: to keep an object, form, symbol, shape or color from becoming dominant; to subjugate, a weak statement

value: color; tint

varnish: a liquid composition containing copal or damar resin used to protect the surface of a painting

wash: a large passage of transparent paint thinned with painting medium

warm colors: as opposed to cool colors; red, yellow and orange

COMPOSITION CHECKPOINTS

STRUCTURE

1. The structure should assume the total available space.
2. Tie the structure letters to the periphery lines.
3. Do not make a contradictory line statement, keeping either parallel or diagonal emphasis dominant.
4. Subjugate all structure and rhythm letters to the main structure letter.
5. Keep rhythm letters subservient to the structure letters.
6. Seek equalization of the lights and darks of the structure pattern.
7. Do not allow disintegration of the structure when applying the motif.

POSITIVE AND NEGATIVE SHAPE

1. Avoid triangles, funnels, pyramids, perfect circles and symmetrical shapes.
2. A form must represent more than one half an object—explain the shape.
3. Repetitious and monotonous shapes should be avoided.
4. Eliminate all negative space—enclose all space with line, texture or color.
5. Background must be held in a positive shape.
6. Do not allow line or motif to strike into the corners of a painting.

FOCAL POINT

1. The focal point should be both the entrance and exit of a painting.
2. The focal point should be placed right or left of the center front.
3. The focal point directs the eye to the point of interest.
4. The focal point should be the strongest color on the painting surface.
5. The focal point color is repeated at least three times in the rhythm pattern.

COLOR
1. Color must be organized in a rhythmic pattern.
2. Keep strong color away from the periphery lines.
3. Keep strong color away from corners.
4. The strongest color in the painting should dominate the center area and the focal point position.

LANDSCAPES
1. Avoid funneling rivers and roads and fields.
2. Always identify more than half an object.
3. Concentrate the drama of the motif in the middle ground.
4. The strongest color should be in the center areas.
5. Do not fill edges and corners with paraphernalia.
6. Eliminate objects not necessary to explain the motif idea.
7. Always use a point of reference for size.
8. Limit the theme to one subject idea.

STILL LIFE
1. Do not mix items of different periods in the same still life.
2. Do not choose bric-a-brac or pieces of ceramic statuary.
3. Avoid using contrived objects such as back drapes.
4. Never place one object directly above another.
5. Unite and/or overlap the objects.
6. Always show more than half an object.
7. Avoid monotonous placement of objects.
8. Avoid monotonous shapes.
9. Do not fill edges and corners with trivia.
10. Design the objects in a rhythmic pattern.
11. Eliminate unnecessary objects of the motif.
12. Hold the background in positive shape.
13. A vase should consume at least one third to one half of the space allotted to a flower motif.
14. Preference must be given to the simple, classic object shapes.

HEAD AND FIGURE
1. Do not allow contour of the head or figure to create negative area.
2. Maintain the head as an oval and the neck as a cylinder.
3. Do not overlap heads.
4. The head must be designed in repose.
5. Place the model in a position that will insure a continuity of contour line.
6. Lighting should be directed from one side *only*.
7. Do not cut the figure with objects such as furniture or cloth.
8. Avoid jewelry, pipes, glasses, unnecessary accessories.
9. Keep the figure relaxed.
10. Do not cut figures off at elbows, wrists, waist or the knees.
11. Always indicate both hands.
12. Keep the appendages from protruding from the body and creating negative space.
13. Avoid props depicting period designs.